Performing Ṣalāh Using the Prophetic Example

Based on Authentic Ḥadīths from the Six Most Authentic Books

صَلُّوا كَمَا رَأَيْتُمونِي أُصَلِّي

"Pray as you have seen me praying." (Bukhārī)

SUMMARY EDITION

M. Mushfiqur Rahman

First Edition: April, 2015 (*Jumādā al-Ākhir*, 1436)

ISBN-10: 1-943108-02-1 (*Summary Edition*)
ISBN-13: 978-1-943108-02-2

ISBN-10: 1-943108-00-5 (main book, color)
ISBN-13: 978-1-943108-00-8

ISBN-10: 1-943108-01-3 (main book, black & white)
ISBN-13: 978-1-943108-01-5

Published by:

FITRAH PRESS
www.fitrahpress.com
info@fitrahpress.com

For order information, feedback, or publishing contracts, including translation into other languages, please write to info@fitrahpress.com.

Ṣalāh

What would life be like without the ṣalāh.
Perhaps no sense of shame for doing something wrong,
Without having to raise the hands soon after,
Saying "Allāhu Akbar – I place the highest priority in
Your obedience";
Nor any sense of security and comfort,
Without being able to place the head on the ground
And leaving all the troubles and worries in Your Hand,
A very personal and intimate Walī, and the Best of all protectors.

Perhaps the days will be passed in pursuit of worldly affairs,
Or in mitigating them,
With little or no remembrance of You.
And without Your remembrance and worship life
will have no meaning,
Other than to consume the moments
And inching towards the time of departure.
It will be a soul with a deep void,
And a life full of depression,
For the human soul finds no tranquility in a body
That lives by instincts and desires.

Without ṣalāh, there will be no vertical bond with the Creator,
A bond that is re-established time and again throughout the day,
Nourishing the soul;
A bond without which I will surely loose my equilibrium
Amidst all the chaos, dogmas, and desires that life brings.

It is a gift, a priceless one, from You;
Without it, life will have no worth.
Thank You for this blessing. Thank You for giving the ability
To place the head down on the ground in submission to You,
For not everyone has been given this blessing.

TRANSLITERATION TABLE

Consonants. Arabic

Initial: unexpressed medial and final:

ء	'	د	d	ض	ḍ	ك	k
ب	b	ذ	dh	ط	ṭ	ل	l
ت	t	ر	r	ظ	ẓ	م	m
ث	th	ز	z	ع	ʿ	ن	n
ج	j	س	s	غ	gh	ه	h
ح	ḥ	ش	sh	ف	f	و	w
خ	kh	ص	ṣ	ق	q	ي	y

Vowels, diphthongs, etc.

short:	ـَ	a	ـِ	i	ـُ	u
long:	ـَا	ā	ـِي	ī	ـُو	ū
diphthongs:	ـَوْ	aw				
	ـَيْ	ay, ai				

CONTENTS

Table of Figures 10
Forewards to the Complete Set 11
Preface 15

First Considerations when Studying the Prophet's Ṣalāh 17
  A. Sincerely Seeking the Most Authentic and Being Consistent 17
  B. Avoiding Pains and Keeping the Right Priorities 17
  C. Multiple Options and Maintaining Balance in Them 18

Intention, Facing the *Qiblah*, and Standing for Ṣalāh 20
  Intention for Ṣalāh (النية لصلاة) 20
  Facing the *Qiblah* (القبلة) 20
  Standing for Ṣalāh (القيام) 21
    Obligatory Prayers While Sitting or Lying Down 22
    Making Non-Obligatory Prayers While Sitting 22
    Distance Between the Feet 23
    Half the Reward of Standing 25
    Switching Between Sitting and Standing 25

Opening *Takbīr*, Placement of the Hands, Fixing the Gaze 28
  Saying the Opening *Takbīr* (تكبيرة الاحرام) 28
    Saying the Opening *Takbīr* when Following an *Imām* 28
  Following the *Imām* in All Actions in Ṣalāh 29
    Consequence of Going Ahead of the *Imām* 30
  Raising the Hands when Saying *Allāhu Akbar* 30
    How High to Raise the Hands 31
  Placing the Hands on the Chest 33
    Placing the Right Hand over the Left 34
    No Evidence: Leaving the Hands Hanging at the Sides 35
    Intertwining the Arms or the Fingers 35
  Fixing the Gaze at the Place of *Sajdah* 35

Opening *Du'ā'*, *Ta'awwudh* and *Basmalah* 40
  The Opening *Du'ā'* (دعاء الإفتتاح) 40
    Opening *Du'ā'* Only in the First *Rak'ah* 42
  Recitation of the *Ta'awwudh* (التعوذ) 42

Recitation of the *Basmalah* (البسملة) 43
Basmalah to Be Recited Quietly 44

Recitation of the Fātiḥah (الفاتحة) 47
Fātiḥah Is Required for Ṣalāh 47
Fātiḥah Should Be Recited in Every *Rak'ah* 47
Reciting the Fātiḥah when Following an *Imām* 48
Āmeen to Be Loud 49
Arguments Against Saying *Āmeen* Loudly 50
Elongating the *Āmeen* 50
Āmeen to Be Said Simultaneously with the *Imām* 51
Virtues of *Āmeen* 52

Recitation From the Qur'ān 54
Qur'ān Recitation in the 1st and the 2nd *Rak'ah* 54
Qur'ān Recitation in the 3rd and the 4th *Rak'ah* 55
Reciting a Complete *Sūrah* in a *Rak'ah* 55
Reciting Multiple *Sūrahs* in a *Rak'ah* 56
Reciting Part of a *Sūrah* in a *Rak'ah* 56
Minimum Amount of Recitation 57
Recitation Is Shorter in the Subsequent *Rak'ahs* 58
Recitation when Following an *Imām* 59
Recitations of the Prophet (s) in Various Prayers 59
Virtues of Specific *Sūrahs* and Verses 61
Order of Recitation 66
Beautifying the Recitation 67
Best Ṣalāh Is One with Long Recitation 68
Consideration for the Weak, the Old, and the Children 68
Audible and Quiet Prayers 69
Tongue Must Be Moved During Quiet Recitations 70

The *Rukū'* (الركوع) 74
Saying the *Takbīr* Before Going to *Rukū'* 74
Raising the Hands Before Going to *Rukū'* 74
Arguments Against Raising the Hands Before Going to *Rukū'* 76
Manner of Performing *Rukū'* 76
Hands on the Knees 76

Hands and Knees Should Support the Weight of the Body 76
Grasping the Knees, Fingers Spaced out Below the Knees 77
Arms Should Be Away from the Sides 77
Back and Head to Be Kept Straight 78
Where to Look when in *Rukūʿ* 78
Allowing the Body to Come to Full Rest in *Rukūʿ*, *Sajdah*, *Qawmah*, *Jalsah*, etc. 81
Ṣalāh Not Valid If *Rukūʿ*, *Sajdah*, etc. Are Not Done Properly 82
Length of Time While in *Rukūʿ*, *Sajdah*, *Qawmah*, and *Jalsah* 83
Recitation in the *Rukūʿ* 83
When Recitations in *Rukūʿ* and *Sajdah* Were Initiated 84
Recitation in *Rukūʿ* and *Sajdah* to Be Done Three Times 85
No Qur'ān Recitation in *Rukūʿ* or *Sajdah* 85

Standing up from the *Rukūʿ* (القومة) 88
Raising the Hands when Rising from the *Rukūʿ* 88
Allowing the Body to Come to Full Rest While Standing 88
Length of Time While Standing 89
Recitation in the *Qawmah:* the *Tasmīʿ* and the *Tahmid* 89
Recitation when Praying Alone or Leading Others as *Imām* 90
Recitation in *Qawmah* when Following an *Imām* 91

The *Sajdah* (السجدة) 93
Excellence of Making *Sajdah* 93
Saying the *Takbīr* when Going to the First *Sajdah* 94
Going to the *Sajdah* – Placing the Hands First 94
Manner of Making the *Sajdah* 97
Making *Sajdah* on "Seven Bones" 97
Forehead and Nose to Touch the Ground 97
Face Should Be Placed Firmly on the Ground 98
Hands to Be Placed on the Ground 98
Position of the Hands on the Ground 99
Fingers to Be Straight Towards the *Qiblah* 100
Elbows to Not Touch the Ground 100
Arms to Be Away from the Sides 101
Thighs to Not Touch Each Other and Be Away from the Belly 101

Feet Vertical and Toes to Face the *Qiblah* 102
Allowing the Body to Come to Full Rest in *Sajdah* 104
Ṣalāh Not Valid If *Sajdah* Is Not Done Properly 104
Length of Time While in *Sajdah* 105
Recitation in the *Sajdah* 105
Recitation in *Sajdah* to Be Done Three Times 106
Making *Duʿā'* While in *Sajdah* 106
No Qur'ān Recitation in *Sajdah* 106

The Sitting in Between the Two *Sajdahs* (الجلسة بين السجدتين) 109
Takbīr when Sitting up from the First *Sajdah* 109
Manner of Sitting Between the *Sujūd* 109
Body Must Come to Full Rest During Sitting Between *Sujūd* 110
Length of Time While Sitting in Between the *Sujūd* 110
Recitation While Sitting in Between the *Sujūd* 111
Saying the *Takbīr* when Going to the Second *Sajdah* 111
Saying the *Takbīr* when Rising from the Second *Sajdah* 112
Briefly Sitting During the Odd *Rakʿahs* (جلسة الإستراحة) 112
Standing up After *Sujūd* or Sitting – Lifting the Knees First 113

The First Sitting (الجلوس الأول) 115
Manner of the First Sitting (افتراش) 115
Recitation in the First Sitting 118
When to Recite the *Tashahhud* 118
Text of the *Tashahhud* 119
Recitations During Sittings Are to Be Done Quietly 119
Raising the Index Finger (الإشارة بالسبابة) 120
Rising from the First Sitting 122
Saying the *Takbīr* when Standing up from the First Sitting 122
Raising the Hands when Standing up from the First Sitting 123

The Final Sitting (الجلوس الأخير) 125
Manner of the Final Sitting (التورك) 125
Arguments Against the *Tawarruk* Sitting 128
Recitations in the Final Sitting 128
The *Tashahhud* 128

Sending Ṣalāh upon the Prophet 129
Importance of Sending Ṣalāh upon the Prophet 129
Text for Sending Ṣalāh upon the Prophet 130
Seeking Refuge in Allāh 131
Text for Seeking Refuge in Allāh 132
Other *Duʿā's* from the Sunnah 133
Making Personal *Duʿā'* 134

Ending the Ṣalāh 137
The *Taslīm* (التسليم) 137
Text of the *Taslīm* 138
Turning Fully to the Right and the Left 139
Whom Do We Address when Saying the *Taslīm* 140
Turning Around and Facing the People 141
Facing the People at a Slight Angle 142
Remaining Sitting for a While After the Ṣalāh 142
Adhkār After Ending the Ṣalāh 143
Counting by the Fingers 144
Making the *Adhkār* Audible 144
Raising the Hands in *Duʿā'* After the Ṣalāh 145

Ṣalāh for Women 147

Bibliography 149

Glossary of Arabic Terms 151

Index 159

TABLE OF FIGURES

Figure 1: Distance Between the Feet 24

Figure 2: Raising the Hands 32

Figure 3: Holding the Hands 37

Figure 4: The *Rukū'* 80

Figure 5: Going to the *Sajdah* 96

Figure 6: Standing up from *Sajdah* or Sitting 96

Figure 7: The *Sajdah* 103

Figure 8: The First Sitting (*Iftirāsh*) 117

Figure 9: The Final Sitting (*Tawarruk*) 127

Figure 10: The *Taslīm* 140

FOREWARDS TO THE COMPLETE SET[1]

(1)

بسم الله الرحمن الرحيم

I had the privilege to review the book *Performing Ṣalāh Using the Prophetic Example* written by Br. Mushfiqur Rahman. It is a book that considered various opinions and *madhāhib* on ṣalāh, but its primary value is that it provides simple, clear, and comprehensive *dalīl* for the performance of ṣalāh from the authentic ḥadīth.

For those who may not be familiar with various *madhāhib* and the source ḥadīths but desire to know how to pray based on the Prophetic example, this book will provide them with that guideline and the confidence that they will be making ṣalāh in the way the Messenger of Allāh (s) prayed. I hope that this book will also be a good guide to be used in Islamic schools, weekend schools, and for the new Muslims.

This book was also reviewed by Shaikh Abdelmoniem Elamin, a well-known scholar of *fiqh* and a teacher in our area, which gives me the confidence that this work has gone through proper revision and review.

May Allāh (swt) reward him for his efforts in this work.

Mohamed Magid
Imam, All Dulles Area Muslim Society (ADAMS Center)
Former President, Islamic Society of North America
Sterling, Virginia
October 28, 2014

[1] The main book and this *Summary Edition.*

(2)

الحمد لله والصلاة والسلام على رسول الله وعلى آله وصحبه أجمعين

Al-ḥamdulillāh, I had the opportunity to review a major portion of the work *Performing Ṣalāh Using the Prophetic Example*. The book systematically categorizes various aspects of the performance of the ṣalāh and brings together the authentic ḥadīths from the six most authentic books of ḥadīths that are available on each topic. *Insha Allāh*, this will enable a reader the opportunity to get to know directly the source ḥadīths on various aspect of the ṣalāh, and also help towards developing an unbiased understanding of the performance of the ṣalāh of the Prophet *ṣalla allāhu ʿalaihi wa sallam* based on authentic ḥadīths. There are obviously some areas that are debatable or where the issue is only a matter of preference. Our great Imams and scholars have differed on these issues, and we remain indebted to them for their invaluable services to the *ummah*. Their opinions, arguments, and elucidation of *fiqhi* issues will continue to remain relevant to us in understanding the Sunnah of the Prophet *ṣalla allāhu ʿalaihi wa sallam*. But having all the source ḥadīths together and being able to examine closely all the texts available can help in minimizing the differences and adopting an option that gives one a level of comfort of following the Prophet *ṣalla allāhu ʿalaihi wa sallam* as closely as possible to the best of his understanding.

One suggestion I will have is to expand this book – perhaps in a future edition – to include a few other books of ḥadīth, such as Imam Mālik's Muwatta' and Musnad Aḥmad. The *Six Most Authentic Books* are very comprehensive in the coverage of the ṣalāh, but adding a few more will, *insha Allāh*, improve it and perhaps bring more clarity on some of the debatable issues.

I hope that this book will benefit many people in their efforts to emulate the ṣalāh of the Prophet *ṣalla allāhu ʿalaihi wa sallam* as best as possible.

Abdelmoniem Elamin
Professor of Islamic Studies and Fiqh, Tooba University
College Park, Maryland
November 22, 2014

(3)

All praise is due to Allāh (swt), and prayers and blessings are upon our beloved Prophet and Guide Muhammad (s).

I had the opportunity to examine the book *Performing Ṣalāh Using the Prophetic Example* by Br. Mushfiqur Rahman. The book cites many ḥadīths and narrations by the *ṣaḥābah* in a very organized fashion, enabling a reader to easily find any topic related to the performance of the ṣalāh. The narrations were cited in detail from the six most authentic books of ḥadīths, including Ṣaḥīḥ Bukhārī and Ṣaḥīḥ Muslim. My sincere opinion is that this book carries a great value.

What makes it unique, however, is that throughout the book, the author focused on the authentic evidence from the original sources. He also highlights the rulings of the different schools of thought and the four Imāms on ṣalāh, and they all point to the same direction, which is the Sunnah of the Prophet (s). We should remember that there is no room for opinion when we have an authentic ḥadīth available on a matter. This was the view of all the four Imāms who have made similar comments to this effect: "When there is an authentic ḥadīth, then that is my *madhhab*, and if my word goes against the word of the Prophet, disregard my word and follow the Prophet (s)."

I am sure that anyone who reads this book with sincerity and an open heart will benefit from it, *insha Allāh*. I highly recommend this book to all the Muslim brothers and sisters around the globe, whether they already know how to make ṣalāh properly or still learning to do so.

Mohamed Abdullahi
Imam, Muslim Community Center
Silver Spring, Maryland
January 13, 2015

إِنَّ الحَمْدَ للهِ نَحْمَدُهُ وَنَسْتَعِينُهُ وَنَسْتَغْفِرُهُ، وَنَعُوذُ بِاللهِ مِنْ شُرُورِ أَنْفُسِنَا وَمِنْ سَيِّئَاتِ أَعْمَالِنَا، مَنْ يَهْدِهِ اللهُ فَلا مُضِلَّ لَهُ، وَمَنْ يُضْلِلْ فَلا هَادِيَ لَهُ، وَأَشْهَدُ أَنْ لا إِلَهَ إِلا اللهُ وَحْدَهُ لا شَرِيكَ لَهُ وَأَشْهَدُ أَنَّ مُحَمَّداً عَبْدُهُ وَرَسُولُهُ

This is the summarized edition of the main volume which bears the same title. The main volume provides comprehensive evidence for all aspects of the performance of the ṣalāh. As a result, it necessarily cites the available authentic narrations from the six most authentic books of ḥadīth[2], engaging often into detail discussions and analysis. While this is useful for serious students who seek comprehensive evidence, it may be overwhelming for the common Muslims who only want to know how to perform the ṣalāh in the most authentic manner based on the prophetic example without delving into detail discussions or having to read all the available ḥadīths on each subject.

It is for them that this easy-to-read abridged edition has been prepared. This edition still includes all the detail elements of the performance of the ṣalāh. However, it avoids full discussions and only includes the conclusions from the main book supported by minimal number of ḥadīths. Hopefully, this will make it simpler and easier for the laymen and the ordinary Muslims to know how to perform the ṣalāh based on the example of the Messenger of Allāh (s).

For those who are interested in knowing why we felt the need to write a new book on ṣalāh when there are many other books already available on it, which books of ḥadīth were consulted and why, and what methodologies were employed in this work, are advised to read the *Introduction* in the main book where these points were addressed at some length. The main book also includes a chapter on achieving *khushūʿ* in ṣalāh and another detailed chapter on the issue *of taqlīd*, or blindly following a particular scholar or school of thought.

---

[2] These are: Bukhārī, Muslim, Abū Dāwud, Tirmidhī, Nasā'ī, and Ibn Mājah.

Additionally, the reader should note the following:

- **Unless explicitly stated to be otherwise, all ḥadīths cited are authentic (*ṣaḥīḥ*).** When a ḥadīth is reported in multiple books, the text is taken from the first book mentioned in the parenthesis.
- The ḥadīth citations in the footnote include the name(s) of the ḥadīth book(s), the chapter name in short form, and the ḥadīth number.
- Key Arabic texts relevant to the topic were included in most of ḥadīths cited in order to eliminate doubt about translation quality and bolster reliability and accuracy of the conclusions taken.
- Sometimes colors were added to key texts that are the focus of the discussion, making them stand out to the reader and help him/her with quick reading. In some cases, colors were also added to an Arabic word in the text of a *duʿā'* or *dhikr* to point to minor variation of this *duʿā'* or *dhikr* in other narrations on or around that particular place.

We ask Allāh (swt) to forgive our sins, shortcomings, and errors. We ask Him to accept this work, grant His blessings in it and make it beneficial for everyone who reads it. May He reward all those who directly or indirectly contributed to this work and grant them well-being and success in this world and the Next.

سبحانك اللهم وبحمدِك أشهدُ أن لا إله إلا أنت أستغفرُك وأتوبُ إليك

M. Mushfiqur Rahman
mushfiqurrahman@hotmail.com
Waldorf, Maryland, USA
Rabīʿ ath-Thānī, 1436
January 25, 2015

P.S. Readers' comments and feedback are welcome. We also request them to inform us of any mistakes or errors done in this work, whether in citations, omissions, analysis, or conclusions.

First Considerations when Studying the Prophet's Ṣalāh

Before undertaking a study of how to make ṣalāh authentically based on the example of the Prophet (s), one should consider a number of points.

A. Sincerely Seeking the Most Authentic and Being Consistent

- **Sincerity**: Every Muslim man and woman should desire to make ṣalāh according to how the Messenger of Allāh (s) performed his ṣalāh or what he instructed the Companions regarding the ṣalāh.
- **Being in the state of learning**: A Muslim should always be in the process of learning and improving his knowledge, understanding, and practice of Islam.
- **Courage to accept corrections and improve**: If one realizes that he was doing a certain aspect of the ṣalāh incorrectly and later comes to know the proper or more correct way of doing it, then his sincerity and commitment to Islam should motivate him to start practicing the correct position without hesitation.

B. Avoiding Pains and Keeping the Right Priorities

- **Physical condition**: If one has any physical condition that makes it difficult or painful to practice a certain posture in the authentic manner, then he should practice an alternative position that is next in preference. Otherwise, his *khushū*ʿ in ṣalāh, an important priority, may be compromised.

> Narrated ʿAbdullāh (bin ʿAbdullāh ibn ʿUmar): I saw ʿAbdullāh ibn ʿUmar (r) crossing his legs while sitting in the ṣalāh, and I, a mere

youngster in those days, did the same. Ibn ʿUmar forbade me to do so and said, "The proper way is to keep the right foot propped up and bend the left in the ṣalāh." I said, "But you are doing so (i.e., crossing your legs)." He said, "My feet cannot bear my weight." (Bukhārī)[1]

This shows great wisdom of Ibn ʿUmar (r). He avoided the Prophetic posture that was painful for him as a result of a physical condition which perhaps affected his concentration in ṣalāh. However, he urged his son to follow the example of the Prophet (s) since it was not difficult for him. This is not laxity, but rather insight and sound understanding of the priorities of the *deen*.

- **Understanding the priorities**: Understanding where to put the priorities is an essential quality of every Muslim, and it is especially important in the acts of *ʿibādah.* One who does not know the right priorities can focus on a peripheral issue while ignoring a required, and hence more important, obligation. For example, if one does not have proper *ṭahārah* (purification) of the body, clothes, or the place of ṣalāh, then there is little use in trying to make the postures correctly since his ṣalāh itself may be invalid.

C. Multiple Options and Maintaining Balance in Them

- **Multiple Options**: Sometimes, there is more than one way of performing an aspect of ṣalāh and each one has evidence in the ḥadīth. The most preferred option may only be obtained after reviewing all the available ḥadīths on the issue. An example would be whether to sit in *Iftirāsh* or *Tawarruk* manner in the final sitting. The preferred option, based on the evidence, is the latter.

- **Some options are almost equally valid**: There are some cases where the Prophet (s) practiced two options and each one has supporting authentic narrations by the Companions. In such cases, one should practice both options regularly. An example of this is saying *rabbanā laka-l-ḥamd* or *rabbanā wa laka-l-ḥamd* when standing up after the *rukūʿ*. Both options are supported by a large number of *ṣaḥīḥ* ḥadīths by multiple Companions.

- **One most preferred option**: In other cases where there are multiple options proven from the Sunnah, a review of the ḥadīths may show that only one option was practiced by the Prophet (s) on a regular basis whereas the other option may be an occasional practice since it is supported by very few narrations, if not just a single ḥadīth. One should, therefore, do the same and not perform an option all the time that was not a regular practice of the Prophet (s). An example of this would be the *Jalsatu-l-Istirāḥah* or the "sitting of rest" in the odd *rakʿahs* before getting up. Although there are a few narrations that support this, the evidence suggests that it was not always practiced by the Prophet (s).
- **Not all options may be the same**: It would be naïve to think that all options are equally valid and should be practiced equally or arbitrarily to show "open mindedness." For instance, adding "wa barakātuh" at the end of the first *taslīm* when ending the ṣalāh. There is a ḥadīth about this, but it is categorized as *ḥasan*. Further, it is narrated by a single Companion. On the other hand, an overwhelming number of authentic narrations by many Companions show that the Prophet (s) used to say *as-salāmu ʿalaikum wa raḥmatullāh* both on the right and the left side on a regular basis.
- **Avoiding assumptions**: It is also important to point out that not all variant practices may have evidence in the Sunnah. One, therefore, should not practice a position that he observes others doing with the assumption that the Messenger of Allāh (s) did the same. An example is leaving the hands hanging on the sides after the opening *takbīr* and not holding them and placing them on the body, a practice that lacks textual evidence in the ḥadīth.

---

[1] Bukhārī, *Adhān*, 827.

Intention, Facing the *Qiblah*, and Standing for Ṣalāh

Intention for Ṣalāh (النية لصلاة)

- **Intention required**: All the four schools of thought agree that intention is required before starting the ṣalāh.[1]

> ʿUmar ibn al-Khaṭṭāb narrated that the Prophet (s) said, "The reward of deeds depends upon the intention and every person will get the reward according to what he has intended ..." (Bukhārī, Muslim)[2]

- **Need not be spoken**: The four schools also agree that intention need not be pronounced as it is a matter of the heart.[3] The Prophet (s) and his Companions (r) never uttered their intentions.
- Ibn Qayyim (r) said:

> The intention – it is the aim and purpose of performing some action. It is a condition of the heart, and it does not come from the tongue. That is why the Prophet (s) and his Companions never spoke their intentions.[4]

- For more discussions on this topic, see *Intention for Ṣalāh* on page 34 in the main book.

Facing the *Qiblah* (القبلة)

- **Required for obligatory ṣalāh**: Facing the *qiblah* when making ṣalāh is obligatory unless one is making voluntary ṣalāh on a mount or transportation. The ḥadīth about this is *mutawātir*.[5]

Jābir (r) narrated: "Allāh's Messenger (s) used to offer ṣalāh (voluntary prayers) while riding on his mount wherever it turned, and whenever he wanted to offer the compulsory ṣalāh, he dismounted and prayed facing the *qiblah* (فاستقبل القبلة)." (Bukhārī)[6]

Abū Hurairah (r) narrated a ḥadīth in which the Prophet (s) instructed a man who did not pray properly by saying: "When you stand up to offer ṣalāh, perform *wuḍū'* properly, then turn to face the *qiblah* (استقبل القبلة) and say the *takbīr* ..." (Muslim)[7]

- **Scholars' opinions**: All the four schools of thought agree that facing the *qiblah* is required for the ṣalāh to be valid.[8]
- For more discussion on this topic, see *Facing the Qiblah* on page 34 in the main book.

Standing for Ṣalāh (القيام)

- **Required for obligatory ṣalāh**: A significant part of ṣalāh is done while standing. Standing is such an important aspect of this pillar of Islam that ṣalāh is sometimes referred to as "standing" (*al-qiyām*).
- **Non-obligatory ṣalāh**: However, when it comes to non-obligatory prayers, one may pray sitting or pray on mount (or transportation) regardless of which direction it turns to.[9]

'Abdullāh ibn 'Umar (r) narrated: "Allāh's Messenger (s) used to offer optional ṣalāh on the back of his mount facing any direction and also used to offer the Witr on it but never offered the prescribed ṣalāh on it." (Bukhārī, Muslim, Abū Dāwud)[10]

Jābir (r) narrated: "Allāh's Messenger (s) used to offer ṣalāh (voluntary prayers) while riding on his mount wherever it turned, and whenever he wanted to offer the compulsory ṣalāh, he dismounted and prayed facing the *qiblah*." (Bukhārī)[11]

- **Scholars' opinions**: According to the Mālikī, Ḥanafī, and Shāfi'ī schools, one cannot perform obligatory ṣalāh sitting on a mount (or transportation) unless one has a legitimate excuse, such as sickness that makes standing difficult, being in war, danger of being harmed on the ground, etc.[12]
- For more evidence and discussion on this, see *Standing Is Required for Obligatory Prayers* on page 36 in the main book.

Obligatory Prayers While Sitting or Lying Down

- **While sitting**: Although obligatory prayers require standing, when one is sick which makes it difficult to stand, he is allowed to make obligatory prayers while sitting until he is able to stand again.

> Anas bin Mālik (r) narrated: "Once Allāh's Messenger (s) rode a horse and fell down and the right side was injured. He offered one of the prayers while sitting (فصلى صلاة من الصلوات وهو قاعد) ..." (Bukhārī, Muslim, Abū Dāwud, Ibn Mājah, Nasā'ī, Tirmidhī)[13]

- **While lying down**: If one is unable to sit, then he may even pray lying down.

> 'Imrān bin Ḥuṣayn (r) narrated: I had piles, so I asked the Prophet (s) about the ṣalāh. He said, "Offer ṣalāh standing and if you cannot do that, offer ṣalāh sitting (فإن لم تستطع فقاعدا), and if you cannot do even that, then offer ṣalāh lying on your side (فإن لم تستطع فعلى جنب)." (Bukhārī, Abū Dāwud, Ibn Mājah, Tirmidhī)[14]

- For more evidence on this, see *Obligatory Ṣalāh While Sitting or Lying Down* on page 41 in the main book.

Making Non-Obligatory Prayers While Sitting

- **Non-obligatory prayers only**: One may make non-obligatory prayers – be that voluntary or Witr – while sitting without any legal excuse.

ʿĀ'isha (r) narrated: "Allāh's Messenger (s) (in his last days) used to offer (night) ṣalāh sitting (كان يصلي جالسا) ..." (Bukhārī)[15]

ʿĀ'isha (r) narrated: "The Messenger of Allāh (s) used to pray for a long time at night. If he prayed standing, he would make *rukūʿ* from a standing position, and if he prayed sitting, he would make *rukūʿ* from a sitting position (وإذا صلى قاعدا ركع قاعدا)." (Muslim, Ibn Mājah)[16]

- For more evidence on this, see *Making Non-Obligatory Prayers While Sitting* on page 41 in the main book.

Distance Between the Feet

- **No textual reference**: The *Six Most Authentic Books*, do not contain any ḥadīth about how far apart the feet should be when one is standing in the ṣalāh.
- **Natural distance for proper balance**: Since there is no textual reference available on this issue, this indicates that the Law-Giver (swt) has left it to each person to maintain a distance between the feet that is natural to him and gives him proper balance and posture. Imposition of any fixed distance irrespective of one's height and size could compromise one's balance and affect his concentration in ṣalāh.
- **Proper emphasis**: Rather than on the distance between one's feet, the emphasis given in the Sunnah is on keeping the rows straight and leaving no gaps in between each other.

Anas bin Mālik (r) narrated: The Prophet (s) said, "Straighten your rows, for I see you from behind my back." Anas added, "Everyone of us used to put his shoulder with the shoulder of his companion (يُلْزِقُ مَنْكِبَهُ بِمَنْكِبِ صَاحِبِهِ) and his foot with the foot of his companion (وقَدَمَهُ بِقَدَمِهِ)." (Bukhārī)[17]

An-Nuʿmān bin Bashīr (r) narrated: The Messenger of Allāh (s) turned around to face the people and said, "Establish the rows," three times, "I swear by Allāh! You will of a surety establish the rows or else Allāh will cause differences among your hearts." So, I saw a person attach his shoulder to the shoulder of his companion (يُلْزِقُ مَنْكِبَهُ بِمَنْكِبِ صَاحِبِهِ) and his knee with his companion's knee (وَرُكْبَتَهُ بِرُكْبَةِ صَاحِبِهِ) and his heel with his companion's heel (وَكَعْبَهُ بِكَعْبِهِ). (Abū Dāwud)[18]

- **Scholars' opinions**: The Mālikī and Ḥanbalī schools have a similar opinion on this. According to these schools, the recommended approach is to be moderate so that the feet are neither too close nor too far apart, based on commonly accepted standards.[19]
- For more evidence and discussion on this, see *Distance Between the Feet* on page 37 in the main book.

Figure 1: Distance Between the Feet

Incorrect practices, or practices that do not have any textual evidence

- A gap that is too close or too wide for comfort.
- Any fixed amount of gap irrespective of the person's height and size.

Half the Reward of Standing

- **Reduced reward**: When one performs ṣalāh while sitting, he gets half the reward of performing it while standing, and when he does it while lying down, he gets half the reward of making ṣalāh while sitting.

> Anas bin Mālik (r) narrated: The Messenger of Allāh (s) went out and saw some people praying while sitting down. He said, "The ṣalāh of one who sits down is equivalent to half of the ṣalāh of one who stands (صلاة القاعد على النصف من صلاة القائم)." (Ibn Mājah)[20]

> ʿImrān bin Ḥuṣayn (r) narrated: I asked Allāh's Messenger (s) about the offering of ṣalāh of a man while sitting. He said, "If he offers ṣalāh while standing it is better, and he who offers ṣalāh while sitting gets half the reward of one who offers ṣalāh standing (نصف أجر القائم), and whoever offers ṣalāh while lying gets half the reward of one who offers ṣalāh while sitting (نصف أجر القاعد)." (Bukhārī, Abū Dāwud, Ibn Mājah, Nasā'ī, Tirmidhī)[21]

- For more evidence on this, see *Half the Reward of Standing* on page 50 in the main book.

Switching Between Sitting and Standing

- **Switching in night ṣalāh**: ʿĀ'isha (r) narrated a number of ḥadīths in which she stated that the Messenger of Allāh (s) would offer *tahajjud* ṣalāh while sitting, and then would stand up to complete his recitation and go into *rukūʿ*.

> ʿĀ'isha (r) narrated: "I never saw the Messenger of Allāh (s) offering the night ṣalāh while sitting except in his old age. He used to re-

cite while sitting (فكان يقرأ قاعدا) and whenever he wanted to make *rukū'*, he would stand up and recite (قام فقرأ) thirty or forty verses and then make *rukū'*." (Bukhārī, Muslim, Nasā'ī, Abū Dāwud, Ibn Mājah)[22]

'Alqamah bin Waqqāṣ said: "I said to 'Ā'isha, 'What did the Messenger of Allāh (s) do in the two *rak'ahs* when he was sitting (وهو جالس)?' She said, 'He used to recite in them, then when he wanted to make *rukū'*, he stood up and made *rukū'* (قام فركع).' " (Muslim, Abū Dāwud)[23]

- For more evidence on this, see *Switching Between Sitting and Standing* on page 42 in the main book.

---

1 Al-Jazīrī, *Islamic Jurisprudence According to the Four Sunni Schools*, p. 276.

2 Bukhārī, *Revelation*, 1; Muslim, *Leadership*, 4927.

3 Al-Jazīrī, *Islamic Jurisprudence*, pp. 280-81; Muhammad and Mughniyyah, *Prescribed Prayers: A Textbook on Jurisprudence According to the Five Schools of Islamic Law*, pp. 41-42.

4 Ibn Qayyim, *Ighatha al-Lufan*, vol. 1, p. 261.

5 Al-Albānī, *The Prophet's Prayer Described*, p. 2.

6 Bukhārī, *Ṣalāh*, 400.

7 Muslim, *Ṣalāh*, 886.

8 Al-Jazīrī, *Islamic Jurisprudence*, pp. 229-32.

9 Editor's commentary on Tirmidhī, *Ṣalāh*, 411.

10 Bukhārī, *Abridged Prayers*, 1098; Muslim, *Traveller's Prayer*, 1618; Abū Dāwud, *Traveler's Prayer*, 1224.

11 Bukhārī, *Ṣalāh*, 400.

12 Al-Jazīrī, *Islamic Jurisprudence*, 269-70.

13 Bukhārī, *Adhān*, 689; Muslim, *Ṣalāh*, 922; Abū Dāwud, *Ṣalāh*, 601; Ibn Mājah, *Establishing Ṣalāh*, 1238; Nasā'ī, *Leading Ṣalāh*, 833; Tirmidhī, *Ṣalāh*, 361.

[14] Bukhārī, *Abridged Prayers*, 1117; Abū Dāwud, *Ṣalāh*, 952; Ibn Mājah, *Establishing Ṣalāh*, 1223; Tirmidhī, *Ṣalāh*, 372.

[15] Bukhārī, *Abridged Prayers*, 1119.

[16] Muslim, *Traveller's Prayer*, 1700; Ibn Mājah, *Establishing Ṣalāh*, 1228.

[17] Bukhārī, *Adhān*, 725.

[18] Abū Dāwud, *Ṣalāh*, 662.

[19] Al-Jazīrī, *Islamic Jurisprudence*, p. 337.

[20] Ibn Mājah, *Establishing Ṣalāh*, 1230.

[21] Bukhārī, *Abridged Prayers*, 1115; Abū Dāwud, *Ṣalāh*, 951; Ibn Mājah, *Establishing Ṣalāh*, 1231; Nasā'ī, *Qiyām al-Lail*, 1661; Tirmidhī, *Ṣalāh*, 371.

[22] Bukhārī, *Abridged Prayers*, 1118; *Tahajjud*, 1148; Muslim, *Traveller's Prayer*, 1704; Nasā'ī, *Qiyām al-Lail*, 1650; Abū Dāwud, *Ṣalāh*, 953; Ibn Mājah, *Establishing Ṣalāh*, 1227.

[23] Muslim, *Traveller's Prayer*, 1707; Abū Dāwud, *Voluntary Prayers*, 1351.

Opening *Takbīr*, Placement of the Hands, Fixing the Gaze

Saying the Opening *Takbīr* (تكبيرة الاحرام)

- **Required**: It is required to say the opening *takbīr* (*takbīratu-l-iḥrām*) when starting the ṣalāh, which is the phrase *allāhu akbar* ("Allāh is the Greatest").

> Abū Hurairah (r) narrated: The Prophet (s) said, "When you stand for ṣalāh, say thc *takbīr* (إذا قمت إلى الصلاة فكبر)..." (Bukhārī, Muslim)[1]

> ʿĀ'isha (r) narrated: "The Messenger of Allāh (s) used to start his ṣalāh with the *takbīr* (يستفتح الصلاة بالتكبير) ..." (Muslim)[2]

- **Scholars' opinions**: All the four schools of thought unanimously agree that mentioning the name of Allāh when one begins the ṣalāh is obligatory.[3]
- For more evidence on this, see *Saying the Opening Takbīr* on page 55 in the main book.

Saying the Opening *Takbīr* when Following an *Imām*

- **Required even when following an *imām***: The opening *takbīr* should be recited even when one follows an *imām*.

> Abū Hurairah (r) narrated: The Prophet (s) said, "The *imām* is to be followed. Say the *takbīr* when he says it (فإذا كبر فكبروا) ..." (Bukhārī, Muslim, Abū Dāwud, Ibn Mājah, Nasā'ī)[4]

> Anas bin Mālik (r) narrated: The Prophet (s) said, "*Imām* is meant to be followed, so when he says the *takbīr*, say the *takbīr* (فإذا كبر فكبروا) ..." (Bukhārī, Muslim, Ibn Mājah, Tirmidhī)[5]

- For more evidence on this, see *Saying the Opening Takbīr when Following an Imām* on page 55 in the main book.

Following the *Imām* in All Actions in Ṣalāh

- **Not permissible to go ahead of the *imām***: When one is led by an *imām*, he should perform all ṣalāh actions after the *imām*, not before him. He should not anticipate the next action of the *imām* and make that action before the *imām* does it. There are many narrations available on this. Following are a few among them:

> Abū Hurairah (r) narrated: The Messenger of Allāh (s) said, "The *imām* has been placed in order that he be followed. Therefore, when he says the *takbīr*, you should say the *takbīr*, and do not say the *takbīr* until he says the *takbīr* (وَلَا تُكَبِّرُوا حَتَّى يُكَبِّرَ). And when he performs *rukū'*, then you perform *rukū'*, and do not make *rukū'* before he makes *rukū'* (وَلَا تَرْكَعُوا حَتَّى يَرْكَعَ) ... and when he makes *sajdah*, you make *sajdah* and do not make *sajdah* until he makes *sajdah* (وَلَا تَسْجُدُوا حَتَّى يَسْجُدَ). And if he prays standing, then you should pray standing, and if he prays sitting, then all of you should pray sitting down as well." (Abū Dāwud)[6]

> Anas bin Mālik (r) narrated: "... when the Prophet (s) finished the ṣalāh with *taslīm*, he said, "The *imām* is appointed to be followed (إنَّما جُعِلَ الإمَامُ لِيُؤتَمَّ بِهِ). So when he says the *takbīr*, say the *takbīr* (فإذا كبر فكبروا), and when he makes *rukū'*, make *rukū'* (وَإذَا رَكَعَ فَارْكَعُوا), and when he rises up, rise up (وإذَا رَفَعَ فَارْفَعُوا), and when he says *sami' allāhu liman ḥamidah*, say *rabbanā wa laka-l-ḥamd*, and when he makes *sajdah*, then make *sajdah* (وَإذَا سَجَدَ فَاسْجُدُوا)." (Bukhārī, Tirmidhī, Ibn Mājah)[7]

- For more evidence and discussion on this, see *Following the Imām in All Actions in Ṣalāh* on page 56 in the main book.

Consequence of Going Ahead of the *Imām*

- **Following the *imām* is required**: Following the *imām* in all actions in the ṣalāh is not a choice but a requirement, and there could be severe consequences for violating this. This is born out by the following ḥadīth narrated by Abū Hurairah (r).

> Abū Hurairah (r) narrated: The Prophet (s) said, "Does the one who raises his head before the *imām* not fear that Allāh may turn his head into the head of a donkey? (Muslim, Bukhārī, Nasā'ī, Tirmidhī)[8]

- **Serious offence**: This ḥadīth shows that going ahead of the *imām* is not a light matter but a serious offence in the sight of Allāh (swt), so much so that the Prophet (s) feared that Allāh (swt) may severely punish one in this life for engaging in such acts.

Raising the Hands when Saying *Allāhu Akbar*

- **When to raise the hands**: One should raise his hands as he says the opening *takbīr*. He may also raise the hands and then say the opening *takbīr*, although the former option of doing it simultaneously seems to have more evidence.

> ʿAbdullāh ibn ʿUmar (r) narrated: "I saw Allāh's Messenger (s) opening ṣalāh with the *takbīr* and raising his hands (فرفع يديه حين يكبر) ..." (Bukhārī, Nasā'ī, Abū Dāwud)[9]

> Abū Ḥumaid as-Sāʿidī (r) narrated: "... I saw him raising both his hands up to the level of the shoulders on saying the *takbīr* (إذا كبر جعل يديه) ..." (Bukhārī, Ibn Mājah)[10]

- **Scholars' opinions**: According to the Ḥanafī school, emulation of the Prophetic Sunnah is to utter the opening *takbīr* while raising the hands.[11]
- For more evidence and discussion on this topic, see *Raising the Hands when Saying Allāhu Akbar* on page 61 in the main book.

How High to Raise the Hands

- **Up to the shoulders**: The following narrations support raising the hands up to the level of the shoulders:

> ʿAbdullāh ibn ʿUmar (r) narrated: "The Messenger of Allāh (s) used to raise both his hands up to the level of his shoulders (حَذْوَ مَنْكِبَيْهِ) when opening the ṣalāh ..." (Bukhārī, Muslim, Abū Dāwud, Ibn Mājah, Nasāʾī, Tirmidhī)[12]

> Abū Hurairah (r) narrated: "When the Messenger of Allāh (s) said the *takbīr* for the ṣalāh, he would raise his hands to shoulder level (حَذْوَ مَنْكِبَيْهِ) ..." (Abū Dāwud)[13]

- **Up to the ears**: There are also narrations that mention that he (s) raised his hands up to the level of the ears. However, narrations that support raising them up to the level of the shoulders are more numerous.

> Mālik bin Ḥuwairith (r) narrated: ... when he (s) "said the *takbīr*, he raised his hands until they were level with his ears (حتّى يُحاذِيَ بهما أذنيه) ..." (Muslim, Abū Dāwud)[14]

> Wā'il bin Ḥujr (r) narrated: ... he (s) "said the *takbīr*, raising both his hands until they were to the level of his ears (حتّى حاذَتا أُذُنَيْهِ) ..." (Abū Dāwud, Ibn Mājah, Nasāʾī)[15]

- **Reconciled option**: A reconciled and preferred way of raising the hands, when saying the *takbīr,* would be to keep the wrists generally at the level of the shoulders with the fingertips reaching somewhere near the ears. According to Imām Nawawī, Imām Shāfiʿī's opinion was to raise the hands at the level of the shoulders with the fingertips reaching the earlobes. "This is how ash-Shāfiʿī' combined the ḥadīth (on this question)," he says.[16]

- For more evidence and discussion on this, see *How High to Raise the Hands* on page 63 in the main book.

Figure 2: Raising the Hands

<u>Incorrect practices, or practices that do not have any textual evidence</u>

- Touching the earlobes when raising the hands.
- Barely raising the hands, then quickly placing them on the body. Some people raise their hands so quickly and so low that their hands do not even reach their chest, let alone the shoulders or the ears. Why not take the time and give Allāh (swt) what is due?
- Fingers bent, or the palms half-way open.

Placing the Hands on the Chest

- **On the chest/above the navel**: After the opening *takbīr*, one should place his hands on the chest or between the navel and the chest.

> Ṭāwus narrated: "The Messenger of Allāh (s) used to place his right hand on his left hand, then grasp both of them on his chest (يشد بينهما على صدره) while he was praying." (Abū Dāwud)[17]

> Jarīr Aḍ-Ḍabbī narrated: "I saw 'Alī, may Allāh be pleased with him, praying while grasping his left hand with his right hand, over the wrist-joint, above the navel (فوق السرة)." (Abū Dāwud, graded *hasan*)[18]

- **No *ṣaḥīḥ* narration for on/below the navel**: There is no authentic ḥadīth in the *Six Most Authentic Books* that mention that the Prophet (s) or any of his Companions (r) placed the hands on or below the navel. Two ḥadīths that mention placing the hands below the navel are both graded *da'eef* (weak).

- **Scholars' opinions**: Imām Shāfi'ī's popular opinion is that the hands should be placed below the chest, and according to another opinion attributed to him, they should be placed on the chest.[19] Although in the Ḥanbalī school the hands should be placed below the navel,[20] according to one narration, Imām Aḥmad's opinion is that they should be placed below the chest.[21] The Mālikī school recommends placing the hands between the navel and the chest.[22] Al-Albānī considers placing them on the chest to be the most authentic and all other narrations supporting contrary opinions to be either "weak or totally baseless."[23]

- For more discussion on this topic, see *Where to Place the Hands* on page 68 in the main book.

Placing the Right Hand over the Left

- **How to place the hands**: When the Messenger of Allāh (s) prayed, he placed his right hand over his left.

> Wā'il bin Ḥujr narrated that he saw the Prophet (s) raise his hands when he started the ṣalāh ... and placed his right hand over his left (وضع يده اليمنى على اليسرى) … (Muslim)[24]

> Sahl bin Saʿd said, "The people were ordered to place the right hand on the left arm (يده اليمنى على ذراعه اليسرى) in ṣalāh." Abū Hazim said, "I knew that the order was from the Prophet (s)." (Bukhārī)[25]

- **Holding/grasping the left hand**: There are narrations available that show that he (s) would grasp or hold the left hand with his right hand beyond merely placing the right hand over the left.

> Wā'il bin Ḥujr (r) narrated: I saw the Prophet (s) performing ṣalāh, and he took hold of his left hand with his right (فأخذ شماله بيمينه). (Ibn Mājah)[26]

> Wā'il bin Ḥujr (r) narrated: "I saw the Messenger of Allāh (s), when he was standing in ṣalāh, grasping his left hand with his right hand (قبض بيمينه على شماله)." (Nasā'ī)[27]

- **Over the wrist-bone**: There are also specific details that mention that he (s) placed his right hand on the back side of his left hand, wrist-bone, and forearm.

> Wā'il bin Ḥujr (r) narrated: "... Then he (s) placed (وَضَعَ) his right hand on the back side of his left palm (على ظهر كفه اليسرى), wrist-bone (والرُّسْغِ), and forearm (والسَّاعِدِ) ..." (Abū Dāwud, Nasā'ī)[28]

- **Scholars' opinions**: All the four schools agree that the right hand should be on the left. According to the Shāfiʿī school in particular, right palm should be over the back of one's left hand while holding onto the left wrist and part of the left forearm.[29]

- For more evidence, see *Placing the Right Hand over the Left* on page 70 in the main book.

No Evidence: Leaving the Hands Hanging at the Sides

There is no ḥadīth in the *Six Most Authentic Books* that show that the Messenger of Allāh (s) ever left his hands hanging on the sides or placed his hands on the left side of the chest. For more discussion on this, see *Leaving the Hands Hanging at the Sides* on page 73 in the main book.

Intertwining the Arms or the Fingers

There is also no evidence for intertwining the arms or the fingers when holding them in ṣalāh. For more discussion on this, see *Intertwining the Arms or the Fingers* on page 74 in the main book.

Fixing the Gaze at the Place of *Sajdah*

- **No explicit text for where to look**: Upon commencing the ṣalāh and subsequently throughout the ṣalāh, one should fix his gaze at the place of the *sajdah*. The *Six Most Authentic Books* do not contain any explicit text regarding where to look at during the ṣalāh. Although there is no text prohibiting looking straight ahead, place of the *sajdah* appears to be the most preferred position based on indirect evidence from a number of ḥadīths.

- **Looking here and there prohibited**: The Messenger of Allāh (s) prohibited looking here and there during ṣalāh, which is a way for the Satan to take away a portion of one's ṣalāh.

> ʿĀ'isha (r) narrated: I asked the Messenger of Allāh (s) about looking hither and thither (عن الا لتفات) in ṣalāh. He replied, "It is a way of stealing by which Satan takes away (a portion) from the ṣalāh of a person." (Bukhārī, Nasā'ī, Tirmidhī)[30]

- **Looking up prohibited**: The Messenger of Allāh (s) also prohibited looking up at the sky during ṣalāh.

Anas bin Mālik (r) narrated: The Prophet (s) said, "What is wrong with those people who look towards the sky (أبصارهم إلى السماء) during ṣalāh?" His tone grew stern while delivering this speech and he said, "They should stop (looking towards the sky), otherwise their eyesight would be snatched away." (Bukhārī, Nasā'ī, Abū Dāwud, Ibn Mājah)[31]

- **Scholars' opinions**: According to the Ḥanbalī school, the Sunnah is to keep one's gaze fixed at the place of *sajdah* while standing in ṣalāh.[32] All the four schools of thought consider it undesirable to close one's eyes during ṣalāh unless it serves a specific purpose.[33]
- For more evidence and discussion on this topic, see *Fixing the Gaze at the Place of Sajdah* on page 74 in the main book.

Figure 3: Holding the Hands

<u>Incorrect practices, or practices that do not have any textual evidence</u>

- Intertwining the arms or the fingers.
- Holding the elbows and placing the arms across the chest.
- Leaving the hands hanging on the sides without placing them on the body.

---

[1] Bukhārī, *Adhān*, 757; Muslim, *Ṣalāh*, 868.

[2] Muslim, *Ṣalāh*, 1110.

[3] Al-Jazīrī, *Islamic Jurisprudence*, p. 288.

[4] Bukhārī, *Adhān*, 734; Muslim, *Ṣalāh*, 930; Abū Dāwud, *Ṣalāh*, 603; Ibn Mājah, *Establishing Ṣalāh*, 846; Nasā'ī, *Commencement of Ṣalāh*, 922.

[5] Bukhārī, *Ṣalāh*, 378; Muslim, *Ṣalāh*, 921; Ibn Mājah, *Establishing Ṣalāh*, 1238; Tirmidhī, *Ṣalāh*, 361.

[6] Abū Dāwud, *Ṣalāh*, 603-04.

[7] Bukhārī, *Adhān*, 805, 732; *Abridged Prayers*, 1114; Tirmidhī, *Ṣalāh*, 361; Ibn Mājah, *Establishing Ṣalāh*, 1238.

[8] Muslim, *Ṣalāh*, 963; Bukhārī, *Adhān*, 691; Nasā'ī, *Leading Ṣalāh*, 829; Tirmidhī, *Travelling*, 582.

[9] Bukhārī, *Adhān*, 738; Nasā'ī, *Commencement of Ṣalāh*, 877; Abū Dāwud, *Ṣalāh*, 741.

[10] Bukhārī, *Adhān*, 828; Ibn Mājah, *Establishing Ṣalāh*, 863.

[11] Al-Jazīrī, *Islamic Jurisprudence*, p. 315.

[12] Bukhārī, *Adhān*, 735-36, 738; Muslim, *Ṣalāh*, 861-63; Abū Dāwud, *Ṣalāh*, 721-22, 742; Ibn Mājah, *Establishing Ṣalāh*, 858; Nasā'ī, *Commencement of Ṣalāh*, 877-79, 1026; Nasā'ī, *At-Taṭbīq*, 1058, 1060; Nasā'ī, *Forgetfulness*, 1183; Tirmidhī, *Ṣalāh*, 255-56.

[13] Abū Dāwud, *Ṣalāh*, 738.

[14] Muslim, *Ṣalāh*, 865; Abū Dāwud, *Ṣalāh*, 726.

[15] Abū Dāwud, *Ṣalāh*, 726; Ibn Mājah, *Establishing Ṣalāh*, 867; Nasā'ī, *Commencement of Ṣalāh*, 880, 890; Nasā'ī, *Forgetfulness*, 1266.

[16] Sabiq, *Fiqh us-Sunnah*, vol. 1, p. 130. In the Ḥanafī school, hands should be raised next to the ears for men and next to the shoulders for women. In the Mālikī and Ḥanbalī schools, hands should be raised at the level of the shoulders. (See Al-Jazīrī, *Islamic Jurisprudence*, pp. 315, 324.) According to Imām Aḥmad, one has the option of raising the hands either to the level of the shoulders or the ears. (See An-Nīmawī, *Athar as-Sunan*, commentary on ḥadīth 314, pp. 160-161.)

[17] Abū Dāwud, *Ṣalāh*, 759.

[18] Abū Dāwud, *Ṣalāh*, 757, graded *ḥasan* by Ibn Abī Shaibah. Al-Albānī graded it *da'eef.*

[19] Abdur-Rahman Ibn Yusuf, *Fiqh al-Imam*, p. 56.

[20] Al-Jazīrī, *Islamic Jurisprudence*, p. 323.

[21] Sabiq, *Fiqh us-Sunnah*, vol. 1, p. 132.

[22] Al-Jazīrī, *Islamic Jurisprudence*, p. 325. In the Ḥanafī school, the hands should be placed below the navel for men and on the chest for women. (See p. 315.)

[23] Al-Albānī, *The Prophet's Prayer Described*, p. 12.

[24] Muslim, *Ṣalāh*, 896.

[25] Bukhārī, *Adhān*, 740 (translation corrected to use "arm" instead of "forearm").

[26] Ibn Mājah, *Establishing Ṣalāh*, 810.

[27] Nasā'ī, *Commencement of Ṣalāh*, 888 (translation corrected to use "grasping" instead of "holding").

[28] Abū Dāwud, *Ṣalāh*, 727; Nasā'ī, *Commencement of Ṣalāh*, 890.

[29] Al-Jazīrī, *Islamic Jurisprudence*, pp. 318, 323, 325-26.

[30] Bukhārī, *Adhān*, 751; Nasā'ī, *Forgetfulness*, 1197-99; Tirmidhī, *Traveling*, 590.

[31] Bukhārī, *Adhān*, 750; Nasā'ī, *Forgetfulness*, 1194; Abū Dāwud, *Ṣalāh*, 913; Ibn Mājah, *Establishing Ṣalāh*, 1044.

[32] Al-Jazīrī, *Islamic Jurisprudence*, p. 323.

[33] *Ibid.*, p. 359.

Opening *Du'ā'*, *Ta'awwudh* and *Basmalah*

The Opening *Du'ā'* (دعاء الإفتتاح)

- **Silence after the opening *takbīr***: The Messenger of Allāh (s) used to be silent for a brief period of time after the opening *takbīr* during which he recited an opening *du'ā'*.

> Samurah bin Jundub (r) narrated: "The Prophet (s) used to pause twice (يسكت سكتتين) in the ṣalāh: once when he started [the ṣalāh] and once when he completed the entire recitation." (Abū Dāwud)[1]

> Abū Hurairah (r) narrated: "Allāh's Messenger (s) used to keep silent between the *takbīr* and the recitation of the Qur'ān (يسكت بين التكبير وبين القراءة), and that interval of silence used to be a short one ..." (Bukhārī, Muslim, Nasā'ī, Abū Dāwud, Ibn Mājah)[2]

- **Option for multiple *du'ā's***: The Messenger of Allāh (s) did not recite one fixed opening *du'ā'* always. There are a number of them that he (s) recited at different times. Some of these are mentioned below:

(1)

اللهمَّ بَاعِدْ بيني وبَينَ خَطايَايَ ، كَما باعَدْتَ بينَ المَشرِقِ والمَغرِبِ ، اللهمَّ نَقِّنِي مِنَ الخَطايَا كَما يُنَقَّى الثَّوْبُ الأبْيَضُ مِنَ الدَّنَسِ ، اللهمَّ اغْسِلْ خَطايَايَ بِالْمَاءِ والثَّلْجِ وَالبَرَدِ

O Allāh, distance between me and my sins as you have distanced between the east and the west. O Allāh, cleanse me of my sins as a white garment is cleaned of dirt. O Allāh, wash my sins with water, ice, and snow. (Bukhārī)[3]

Muslim and Nasā'ī have an identical version[4] except for these changes: a) it uses *ighsilni min khaṭaya* instead of *ighsil khaṭāyāya,* and b) it uses *thalj* before *mā'i* (*bi-th-thalji wa-l-mā'i*). Abū Dāwud and Ibn Mājah also have similar versions of this *du'ā'* with some minor variations.[5]

(2b)

وَجَّهتُ وَجْهِيَ لِلَّذِي فَطَرَ السَّماوَاتِ وَالأرْضَ حَنِيفاً وَما أنا مِنَ المُشْرِكِين ، إنَّ صَلَاتِي وَنُسُكِي وَمَحْيَايَ وَمَماتِي لله رَبِّ العالَمِين ، لا شَرِيكَ لَهُ وَبِذَلِكَ أُمِرْتُ وَأنا أوَّلُ المُسْلِمِين

I have submitted my face in submission to the One Who originated the heavens and the earth, and I am not one of the idolaters. Verily, my ṣalāh, my sacrifice, my living, and my dying are for Allāh, the Lord of the Worlds. He has no partner. And of this, I have been commanded, and I am the first of the Muslims. (Muslim)[6]

(3)

سُبْحَانَكَ اللَّهُمَّ وَبِحَمْدِكَ وَتَبَارَكَ اسْمُكَ وَتَعَالَى جَدُّكَ وَلا إلَهَ غَيْرُكَ

Glory and Praise is to You, O Allāh, blessed is Your Name and Exalted is Your Majesty, and there is no deity worthy of worship except You. (Muslim, Abū Dāwud)[7]

- **Recommendation for new Muslims/*imām***: For a new Muslim convert who is beginning to learn the ṣalāh, this particular version (no. 3) may be recommended since it is shorter than the others. It is also advisable for an *imām* to choose a shorter *du'ā'* when leading ṣalāh out of consideration for the followers.
- For more *du'ā's* as well as their supporting ḥadīths, see *Texts of the Opening Du'ā'* on page 84 in the main book.

Opening *Du'ā'* Only in the First *Rak'ah*

- **In first *rak'ah* only**: The opening *du'ā'* is to be recited once during the first *rak'ah* after starting the ṣalāh and not in the subsequent *rak'ahs*. The following narration from Abū Hurairah (r) indicates that when the Messenger of Allāh (s) began the second *rak'ah*, he immediately started reciting the *Fātiḥah*.

> Abū Hurairah (r) narrated: "When the Messenger of Allāh (s) stood up from the second *rak'ah* (نهض من الركعة الثانية), he would start his recitation with *alḥamdu lillāhi rabbi-l-'ālamīn*, and he did not pause (لم يسكت)." (Muslim)[8]

- **Scholars' opinions**: According to the Ḥanafī and the Shāfi'ī schools, the opening *du'ā'* should be recited in the first *rak'ah* after the opening *takbīr*.[9]

Recitation of the *Ta'awwudh* (التعوذ)

- **The *ta'awwudh***: After the opening *du'ā'*, the Messenger of Allāh (s) would seek refuge in Allāh (swt) from the Satan by reciting the *ta'awwudh*, according to a number of *ḥasan* narrations in the *Six Most Authentic Books*.

- **Option for multiple *adhkār***: He (s) used to recite several forms of the *ta'awwudh* at different times. Some of these are:

(1)

أعوذُ باللّهِ السَّميعِ العليمِ منَ الشَّيطانِ الرَّجيمِ ، مِن همزِهِ ونفخِهِ ونفثِهِ

I seek refuge in Allāh, the All-Hearing, the All-Knowing, from the accursed Satan, from his breath, his spit, and his prodding. (Tirmidhī, Abū Dāwud, both graded *ḥasan*)[10]

(2)

اللَّهُمَّ إنِّي أعوذُ بِكَ منَ الشَّيطانِ الرَّجيمِ ، مِن همزِهِ ونفخِهِ ونفثِهِ

O Allāh, I seek refuge in You from the accursed Satan, from his breath, his spit, and his prodding. (Ibn Mājah, *ḥasan*)[11]

(3)

أعوذُ باللَّه منَ الشَّيطانِ مِن نفخِهِ ونفثِهِ وهمزهِ

I seek refuge in Allāh from the Satan, from his spit, his prodding, and his breath. (Abū Dāwud, *ḥasan*)[12]

- **Scholars' opinions**: According to the Ḥanafī, Shāfiʿī, and Ḥanbalī schools, emulation of the Prophetic Sunnah is to seek Allāh's protection from the Satan in the first *rakʿah* after the opening *duʿā'*. The specific text is *aʿūdhu billāhi min ash-shayṭāni-r-rajīm*. According to the Shāfiʿī school, it is preferable to recite this in every *rakʿah*.[13]
- For additional forms of the *taʿawwudh* and supporting ḥadīths, see *Recitation of the Taʿawwudh* on page 93 in the main book.

Recitation of the *Basmalah* (البسملة)

- **The *basmalah***: The *basmalah* or the *bismillāh* is the following phrase:

  بسم الله الرحمن الرحيم

  In the Name of Allāh, the Most Compassionate, the Most Merciful.

  The Messenger of Allāh (s) would open his ṣalāh with the *basmalah*.

> Nuʿaim al-Mujmir narrated: "I prayed behind Abū Hurairah and he recited *bismillāhi-r-raḥmāni-r-raḥīm*, then he recited (ثم قرأ) the *Ummu-l-Qur'ān* (the *Fātiḥah*) ... And after he had said the *salām*, he said, 'By the One in Whose Hand is my soul, my ṣalāh most closely resembles the ṣalāh of the Messenger of Allāh (s).' " (Nasā'ī)[14]

> ʿAbdullāh ibn ʿAbbās (r) narrated: "The Prophet (s) would open his ṣalāh with (يفتح صلاته) *bismillāhi-r-raḥmāni-r-raḥīm*." (Tirmidhī, graded *ḥasan*)[15]

- For further evidence and discussion on this, see *Recitation of the Basmalah* on page 95 in the main book.

Basmalah to Be Recited Quietly

- **The first thing heard**: When the Companions (r) prayed behind the Messenger of Allāh (s), the first thing they heard him (s) reciting audibly is the *Fātiḥah*. This is a likely indication that he (s) recited the *basmalah* quietly.

> Anas bin Mālik (r) narrated: "The Prophet (s), Abū Bakr, and ʿUmar (r) used to start ṣalāh with (يفتتحون الصلاة ب) *al-ḥamdu lillāhi rabbi-l-ʿālamīn.*" (Bukhārī, Ibn Mājah, Abū Dāwud Tirmidhī)[16]

> ʿĀ'isha (r) narrated: "The Messenger of Allāh (s) used to start his ṣalāh with the *takbīr* and the recitation of (يستفتح الصلاة بالتكبير و القراءة ب) *al-ḥamdu lillāhi rabbi-l-ʿālamīn* ..." (Muslim, Abū Dāwud)[17]

- ***Basmalah* not heard**: In another ḥadīth, Anas bin Mālik (r) specifically mentioned that he did not hear the *basmalah* being recited.

> Anas bin Mālik (r) narrated: "I prayed with the Messenger of Allāh (s) and with Abū Bakr, ʿUmar, and ʿUthmān, and I did not hear any of them (فلم أسمع أحدا منهم) reciting *bismillāhi-r-raḥmāni-r-raḥīm.*" (Muslim, Nasā'ī)[18]

- **Recited, but not out loud**: The above narration does not necessarily mean that the *basmalah* was not recited at all; rather, it was not recited "out loud." This is evident from a different narration of this ḥadīth by Anas bin Mālik (r) in Nasā'ī: where he said, "I did not hear any of them say *out loud* (فلم أسمع أحدا منهم يجهر) *bismillāhi-r-raḥmāni-r-raḥīm.*"[19]

- **Scholars' opinions**: According to Imām Abū Ḥanīfah, the *basmalah* is part of the Qur'ān that was revealed to separate the *sūrahs* but it is not part of the *Fātiḥah* or any particular *sūrah*;

therefore, it should be recited quietly.[20] In fact, in the Ḥanafī school, Prophetic example is to recite the *basmalah* at the beginning of each *rak'ah* whether one is praying alone or leading others and whether it is a loud or quiet ṣalāh.[21] Imām Aḥmad is also of the opinion that the *basmalah* should be recited quietly and in every *rak'ah*.[22]

- For further evidence and discussion on this, see *Basmalah to Be Loud or Quiet* on page 98 in the main book.

---

1 Abū Dāwud, *Ṣalāh*, 778, 780.

2 Bukhārī, *Adhān*, 744; Muslim, *Masājid*, 1354-55; Nasā'ī, *Commencement of Ṣalāh*, 896; Abū Dāwud, *Ṣalāh*, 781; Ibn Mājah, *Establishing Ṣalāh*, 805.

3 Bukhārī, *Adhān*, 744.

4 Muslim, *Masājid*, 1354-55; Nasā'ī, *Commencement of Ṣalāh*, 896.

5 Abū Dāwud, *Ṣalāh*, 781; Ibn Mājah, *Establishing Ṣalāh*, 805.

6 Muslim, *Traveller's Prayer*, 1813.

7 Muslim, *Ṣalāh*, 892; Abū Dāwud, *Ṣalāh*, 776.

8 Muslim, *Masājid*, 1356.

9 Al-Jazīrī, *Islamic Jurisprudence*, pp. 315, 318.

10 Tirmidhī, *Ṣalāh*, 242; Abū Dāwud, *Ṣalāh*, 775, both graded *ḥasan.*

11 Ibn Mājah, *Establishing Ṣalāh*, 807, graded *ḥasan.*

12 Abū Dāwud, *Ṣalāh*, 764-65, graded *ḥasan.*

13 Al-Jazīrī, *Islamic Jurisprudence*, pp. 315, 319, 332-33. In the Mālikī school, it is undesirable to say it in the obligatory prayers but allowed in voluntary prayers. (See Al-Jazīrī, *Islamic Jurisprudence*, p. 333.)

14 Nasā'ī, *Commencement of Ṣalāh*, 906.

15 Tirmidhī, *Ṣalāh*, 245, graded *ḥasan.*

16 Bukhārī, *Adhān*, 743; Ibn Mājah, *Establishing Ṣalāh*, 813; Abū Dāwud, *Ṣalāh*, 782; Tirmidhī, *Ṣalāh*, 246.

17 Muslim, *Ṣalāh*, 1110; Abū Dāwud, *Ṣalāh*, 783.

18 Muslim, *Ṣalāh*, 890-91, 893; Nasā'ī, *Commencement of Ṣalāh*, 907-908.

19 Nasā'ī, *Commencement of Ṣalāh*, 908.

20 Editor's commentary on Tirmidhī, *Ṣalāh*, 246; Al-Jazīrī, *Islamic Jurisprudence*, p. 333.

[21] Al-Jazīrī, *Islamic Jurisprudence*, pp. 315, 333.

[22] *Tafsīr Ibn Kathīr*, vol. 1, p. 62; Al-Jazīrī, *Islamic Jurisprudence*, p. 322. According to Imām Shāfi'ī, since the *basmalah* is part of the *Fātiḥah*, it is obligatory to recite it. It should be recited aloud when the *Fātiḥah* is recited aloud in the ṣalāh. Imām Mālik's opinion, based on the ḥadīth of 'Ā'isha mentioned above, is that the *basmalah* should not be recited – neither loudly, nor silently – when one recites the *Fātiḥah* during the ṣalāh in obligatory prayers, but one may do so in voluntary prayers. (See *Tafsīr Ibn Kathīr*, vol. 1, p. 60, 62; Al-Jazīrī, *Islamic Jurisprudence*, 334; Muḥammad and Mughniyyah, *Prescribed Prayers*, pp. 44-45.)

Recitation of the Fātiḥah (الفاتحة)

Fātiḥah Is Required for Ṣalāh

- **Ṣalāh invalid without it**: Most scholars agree that without the recitation of the *Fātiḥah*, ṣalāh is not valid. There are many ḥadīths available on this, a few of which are mentioned below.

> ʿUbādah bin as-Ṣāmit (r) narrated: Allāh's Messenger (s) said, "There is no ṣalāh (لا صلاة) for one who does not recite *sūrah* al-Fātiḥah in his ṣalāh (i.e., his ṣalāh is invalid)." (Bukhārī, Muslim, Abū Dāwud, Ibn Mājah, Nasā'ī, Tirmidhī)[1]

> Abū Hurairah (r) narrated: The Prophet (s) said, "Whoever offers a ṣalāh in which he does not recite the *Ummu-l-Qur'ān* [al-Fātiḥah], it is deficient (فهي خداج)," repeating it three times, "not complete (غير تمام) ..." (Muslim, Abū Dāwud, Ibn Mājah, Nasā'ī, Tirmidhī)[2]

- **Scholars' opinions**: According to the Mālikī, Shāfiʿī and the Ḥanbalī schools, one must recite the *Fātiḥah* in every ṣalāh, whether it is an obligatory or voluntary ṣalāh. In the Ḥanafī school, the Prophetic example is to recite the *Fātiḥah*, although they consider it only *wājib*, not *farḍ*.[3]

Fātiḥah Should Be Recited in Every *Rakʿah*

- **Recited in every *rakʿah***: Fātiḥah should be recited in every *rakʿah*, not just the first *rakʿah*.

Abū Qatādah (r) narrated: "The Prophet (s) used to recite the *Fātiḥatu-l-Kitāb* and a *sūrah* in the first two *rak'ahs* (الركعتين الأوليين) of Ẓuhr and 'Aṣr, and he would let us hear a verse sometimes, and in the last two *rak'ahs* (الركعتين الأخريين) he would recite al-Fātiḥah (only)." (Muslim, Bukhārī, Abū Dāwud, Nasā'ī)[4]

Abū Hurairah (r) narrated: "The Qur'ān is recited in every ṣalāh ... If you recite *sūrah* al-Fātiḥah only, it is sufficient (أجزأت), but if you recite something else in addition, that would be better." (Statement by Abū Hurairah) (Bukhārī, Muslim)[5]

- **Scholars' opinions**: According to the Mālikī, Shāfi'ī and the Ḥanbalī schools, one must recite the *Fātiḥah* in every *rak'ah*, whether it is an obligatory or voluntary ṣalāh.[6]
- For more evidence on this, see *Fātiḥah Should Be Recited in Every Rak'ah* on page 105 in the main book.

Reciting the Fātiḥah when Following an *Imām*

- **Difference of opinion**: Scholars differ on whether one should recite the *Fātiḥah* when he is following an *imām*.
- **Command to listen**: There are a number of narrations where the Messenger of Allāh (s) said that one should listen attentively when the *imām* recites, while there are other narrations that mention that one should recite the *Fātiḥah* behind the *imām* (perhaps quietly).

Abū Mūsā al-Ash'arī (r) narrated: The Messenger of Allāh (s) said, "When the *imām* recites, then listen attentively (إذا قرأ الإمام فأنصتوا) ..." (Ibn Mājah, Abū Dāwud)[7]

Abū Hurairah (r) narrated: The Messenger of Allāh (s) said, "The *imām* has been appointed to be followed, so when he says *allāhu akbar*, then say *allāhu akbar*, when he recites, then listen attentively (وإذا قرأ فأنصتوا) ..." (Ibn Mājah, Nasā'ī)[8]

> Abū as-Sā'ib reports from Abū Hurairah: The Messenger of Allāh (s) said, "Whoever performs a ṣalāh in which he does not recite *Ummu-l-Qur'ān*, it is deficient, not complete." I said, "O Abū Hurairah, sometimes I am behind the *imām*." He pressed my forearm and said, "O Persian! Recite it to yourself (اقرأ بها في نفسك)." (Ibn Mājah, Muslim, Nasā'ī, Tirmidhī)[9]

- **Listening when following an *imām***: Based on these and other ḥadīths on this subject, the most preferred opinion, perhaps, is that if the *imām* is reciting the Fātiḥah in a loud ṣalāh, then one should listen attentively and not recite the *Fātiḥah*. But if it is a quiet ṣalāh, then the followers should recite the *Fātiḥah*.
- **Scholars' opinions**: According to Al-Albānī (r), the most balanced opinion is to recite the *Fātiḥah* when the *imām* is reciting quietly and just listen when he is reciting aloud.[10] In the Mālikī school also, it is recommended to recite the *Fātiḥah* behind the *imām* if the recitation is quiet but undesirable if it is aloud.[11]
- For more evidence and a thorough discussion on this, see *Recitation when Following an Imām* on page 138 in the main book.

Āmeen to Be Loud

- **Meaning of *Āmeen*:** One should end the recitation of the *Fātiḥah* with saying *āmeen*, which means "O Allāh! Accept our invocation."[12] In other words, by saying *āmeen*, one asks Allāh (swt) to grant him what he has just asked for in the *Fātiḥah*.
- ***Āmeen* to be loud**: Although there is some difference of opinion as to whether the *āmeen* should be said loudly or quietly during the audible prayers, the most correct opinion is to say it loudly.

  The following are among the many narrations that support this:

> Abū Hurairah (r) narrated: The Prophet (s) said, "When the *imām* says *āmeen*, then you (should all) say *āmeen* (إذا أمن الإمام فأمنو), for the angels say *āmeen* at that time, and he whose *āmeen* coincides with the *āmeen* of the angels, all his past sins will be forgiven." (Bukhārī, Muslim, Abū Dāwud, Tirmidhī)[13]

> ʿAlī ibn Abī Ṭālib (r) narrated: "I heard the Messenger of Allāh (s) saying *āmeen* (قال آمين) after he said *wa lā-ḍ-ḍāllīn*." (Ibn Mājah)[14]

> Wā'il bin Ḥujr (r) narrated: "When the Messenger of Allāh (s) used to say *wa lā-ḍ-ḍāllīn*, he would say *āmeen* (قال آمين) and raise his voice with it (ورفع بها صوته)." (Abū Dāwud)[15]

> Wā'il bin Ḥujr (r) narrated: "I heard the Prophet (s) recite *ghairi-l-maghdūbi ʿalaihim wa lā-ḍ-ḍāllīn*, and he said *āmeen* (قال آمين), and he stretched it out with his voice (ومد بها صوته)." (Tirmidhī)[16]

- **Scholars' opinions**: According to the Shāfiʿī and Ḥanbalī schools, *āmeen* should be said loudly in loud prayers and silently in silent prayers.[17]
- For more evidence and a detailed discussion on this, see *Āmeen to Be Loud or Quiet* on page 106 in the main book.

Arguments Against Saying *Āmeen* Loudly

As mentioned above, there are some difference of opinions among the scholars about whether *āmeen* is to be said loudly or silently. The main arguments for saying *āmeen* silently have been addressed in the section *Arguments Against Saying Āmeen Loudly* on page 111 in the main book.

Elongating the *Āmeen*

One should elongate the utterance when saying the *āmeen*. The ḥadīths above not only show that the Prophet (s) said the *āmeen* loudly, but also he (s) "raised his voice with it" and "stretched it out with his voice."

Āmeen to Be Said Simultaneously with the *Imām*

- **When to say the *āmeen***: The Prophet's (s) instruction "when the *imām* says *āmeen*, then you say *āmeen* (إذا أمن الإمام فأمنو)" (see the ḥadīth of Abū Hurairah (r) cited above) likely indicates that the *imām* and the followers should all say *āmeen* at the same time. This interpretation of "when" to mean "at the same time" is evident from the following ḥadīths:

> ʿAlī ibn Abī Ṭālib (r) narrated: "I heard the Messenger of Allāh (s) saying *āmeen* (قال آمين) after he said *wa lā-ḍ-ḍāllīn*." (Ibn Mājah)[18]

> Abū Mūsā al-Ashʿarī (r) narrated: The Messenger of Allāh (s) addressed us and explained our Sunnah to us and taught us our ṣalāh. He said, "... when he (the *imām*) says the *takbīr*, then say the *takbīr*; when he says *ghairi-l-maghdūbi ʿalaihim wa lā-ḍ-ḍāllīn* then say *āmeen* (فقولوا آمين) ..." (Muslim, Abū Dāwud, Nasāʾī)[19]

> Abū Hurairah (r) narrated: The Messenger of Allāh (s) used to teach us saying, "Do not precede the *imām* ... When he says *wa lā-ḍ-ḍāllīn*, say *āmeen* (فقولوا آمين) ..." (Muslim, Ibn Mājah)[20]

These ḥadīths show that both the *imām* and the followers are to say *āmeen* after *wa lā-ḍ-ḍāllīn*, thus indicating that they say it at the same time.

- **Do not say before the *imām* does**: The followers, therefore, should not say *āmeen* before the *imām* does it, as many people do when praying in congregation. When the *imām* says *wa lā-ḍ-ḍāllīn* and elongates it according to the rules of *tajwīd*, it takes a few moments for him to regain his breath. So, it is neessary for the followers to allow a few moments to pass and when the *imām* is ready and says *āmeen*, they should say it at the same time.

- **Scholars' opinions**: According to the Shāfiʿī school, when the recitation is loud, *āmeen* should be said together with the *imām*.[21] Al-Albānī has the same opinion. He says, "The *āmeen* of the congregation behind the *imām* should be done loudly and simultaneously with the *imām*, not before him as majority of worshippers do, nor after him."[22] This is also the opinion of Sabiq.[23]

- For more evidence and discussion on this topic, see *Saying of Āmeen by the Imām and the Followers* on page 109 in the main book.

Virtues of *Āmeen*

- **All sins forgiven**: Saying *āmeen* after reciting the *Fātiḥah* is a virtuous act. According to many ḥadīths, angels also say *āmeen,* and if one's saying of *āmeen* coincides with that of the angels, then Allāh (swt) will forgive his past sins.

> Abū Hurairah (r) narrated: The Prophet (s) said, "Say *āmeen* when the *imām* says it and if the *āmeen* of any one of you coincides with that of the angels (وافق قوله قول الملائكة), then all of his past sins will be forgiven (غفر له ما تقدم من ذنبه)." (Bukhārī, Muslim, Nasā'ī, Abū Dāwud, Tirmidhī)[24]

- For more evidence, see *Virtues of Āmeen* on page 110 in the main book.

---

[1] Bukhārī, *Adhān*, 756; Muslim, *Ṣalāh*, 874-77; Abū Dāwud, *Ṣalāh*, 822-23; Ibn Mājah, *Establishing Ṣalāh*, 837; Nasā'ī, *Commencement of Ṣalāh*, 911-12; Tirmidhī, *Ṣalāh*, 247.

[2] Muslim, *Ṣalāh*, 878-81; Abū Dāwud, *Ṣalāh*, 821; Ibn Mājah, *Establishing Ṣalāh*, 838; Nasā'ī, *Commencement of Ṣalāh*, 910; Tirmidhī, *Tafsīr*, 2953.

[3] Al-Jazīrī, *Islamic Jurisprudence*, p. 297; Muḥammad and Mughniyyah, *Prescribed Prayers*, pp. 44-45. In the Ḥanafī school, recitation of the Fātiḥah is not *farḍ* (obligatory) but a *wājib* (a "duty"), and recitation from any part of the Qur'ān suffices. More specifically, it is *wājib* to recite the Fātiḥah in the first two *rak'ahs* of obligatory prayers and every *rak'ah* of the voluntary prayers. (*Ibid.*, p. 298, 300, 311, 316.)

[4] Muslim, *Ṣalāh*, 1013; Bukhārī, *Adhān*, 776; Abū Dāwud, *Ṣalāh*, 799; Nasā'ī, *Commencement of Ṣalāh*, 978.

[5] Bukhārī, *Adhān*, 772; Muslim, *Ṣalāh*, 884.

[6] Al-Jazīrī, *Islamic Jurisprudence*, p. 297. According to the Ḥanafī school, the *Fātiḥah* is not required for the prayer to be valid and recitation from any part of the Qur'ān suffices. It is, however, *wājib* to recite the *Fātiḥah*. (*Ibid.*, p. 298, 300.)

[7] Ibn Mājah, *Establishing Ṣalāh*, 847; Abū Dāwud, *Ṣalāh*, 973.

[8] Ibn Mājah, *Establishing Ṣalāh*, 846; Nasā'ī, *Commencement of Ṣalāh*, 923.

[9] Ibn Mājah, *Establishing Ṣalāh*, 838; Muslim, *Ṣalāh*, 880; Nasā'ī, *Commencement of Ṣalāh*, 910; Tirmidhī, *Tafsīr*, 2953.

[10] Al-Albānī, *The Prophet's Prayer Described*, p. 104.

[11] Al-Jazīrī, *Islamic Jurisprudence*, p. 299; Editor's commentary on Tirmidhī, *Ṣalāh*, 311. According to the Ḥanafī school, it is undesirable – nearly forbidden – to recite the *Fātiḥah* when following an *imām* since the recitation of the *imām* suffices for the followers, whether it is a quiet or loud prayer. (See Al-Jazīrī, *Islamic Jurisprudence*, p. 299; Sabiq, *Fiqh us-Sunnah*, vol. 1, p. 146.)

[12] Ibn Kathīr, *Tafsīr Ibn Kathīr*, vol. 1, p. 91.

[13] Bukhārī, *Adhān*, 780; *Invocations*, 6402; Muslim, *Ṣalāh*, 915-16; Nasā'ī, *Commencement of Ṣalāh*, 926-27, 929; Abū Dāwud, *Ṣalāh*, 936; Tirmidhī, *Ṣalāh*, 250.

[14] Ibn Mājah, *Establishing Ṣalāh*, 854.

[15] Abū Dāwud, *Ṣalāh*, 932.

[16] Tirmidhī, *Ṣalāh*, 248-49.

[17] Al-Jazīrī, *Islamic Jurisprudence*, p. 325; Al-Misrī, *Reliance of the Traveller*, p. 133. According to Ḥanafī and Mālikī schools, *āmeen* should be said silently at all times. (See Al-Jazīrī, *Islamic Jurisprudence*, p. 325; Al-Albānī, *The Prophet's Prayer Described*, p. 24; Ibn Yusuf, *Fiqh al-Imam*, p. 88.)

[18] Ibn Mājah, *Establishing Ṣalāh*, 854.

[19] Muslim, *Ṣalāh*, 904; Abū Dāwud, *Ṣalāh*, 972-73; Nasā'ī, *Leading Ṣalāh*, 831; *At-Taṭbīq*, 1065, 1173; *Forgetfulness*, 1281.

[20] Muslim, *Ṣalāh*, 932-33; Ibn Mājah, *Establishing Ṣalāh*, 846.

[21] Al-Jazīrī, *Islamic Jurisprudence*, p. 319.

[22] Al-Albānī, *The Prophet's Prayer Described*, 24.

[23] Sabiq, *Fiqh us-Sunnah*, vol. 1, p. 137.

[24] Bukhārī, *Adhān*, 780; Muslim, *Ṣalāh*, 915-16; Nasā'ī, *Commencement of Ṣalāh*, 926-27, 929; Abū Dāwud, *Ṣalāh*, 936; Tirmidhī, *Ṣalāh*, 250.

Recitation From the Qur'ān

After reciting the *Fātiḥah*, the Messenger of Allāh (s) would recite from the Qur'ān.

Qur'ān Recitation in the 1st and the 2nd *Rak'ah*

- **He (s) used to recite in the first two *rak'ahs***: The Prophet (s) would recite from the Qur'ān in the first two *rak'ahs* of the obligatory ṣalāh. He would recite a passage from the Qur'ān or an entire *sūrah*, and sometimes multiple *sūrahs* if it was a voluntary ṣalāh.

> Abū Qatādah (r) narrated: "The Prophet (s) used to recite the *Fātiḥatu-l-Kitāb* and a *sūrah* (وسورة) in the first two *rak'ahs* (في الركعتين الأوليين) of Ẓuhr and 'Aṣr, and he would let us hear a verse sometimes, and in the last two *rak'ahs* he would recite al-Fātiḥah (only)." (Muslim, Nasā'ī)[1]

> Abū Salāmah (r) narrated: "The Messenger of Allāh (s) used to recite the *Ummu-l-Qur'ān* (the *Fātiḥah*) and two *sūrahs* (وسورتين) in the first two *rak'ahs* (في الركعتين الأوليين) of Ẓuhr and 'Aṣr and he would make us hear a verse sometimes, and he used to make the first *rak'ah* of Ẓuhr lengthy, and he did likewise in *Subḥ*." (Nasā'ī)[2]

- **Scholars' opinions**: All the four schools of thought hold that the Prophetic example is to recite a *sūrah* or some passage from the Qur'ān after the *Fātiḥah* in the first two *rak'ahs* of the obligatory prayers.[3]

- For more evidence on this, see *Qur'ān Recitation in the 1st and the 2nd Rak'ah* on page 132 in the main book.
- For ḥadīths on what *sūrahs* the Messenger of Allāh (s) recited in different prayers, see *Recitations of the Prophet (s) in Various Prayers* on page 59 below.

Qur'ān Recitation in the 3rd and the 4th *Rak'ah*

- **Not required in obligatory ṣalāh**: Recitation from the Qur'ān in the 3rd and 4th *rak'ah* of the obligatory ṣalāh is not required. There is no ḥadīth in the *Six Most Authentic Books* showing that the Messenger of Allāh (s) recited Qur'ān in the 3rd and 4th *rak'ah* of the obligatory ṣalāh after he recited the *Fātiḥah.*
- **May be recited in voluntary ṣalāh**: In voluntary prayers, it is Sunnah to recite from the Qur'ān. In a long ḥadīth in Abū Dāwud, Ḥudhaifah (r) narrated that once he prayed *tahajjud* with the Prophet (s) in which he recited *sūrah* al-Baqarah in the first *rak'ah* before going to the *rukū'*. He completed the ḥadīth by saying that in that ṣalāh, the Prophet (s) "prayed four *rak'ahs* in which he recited al-Baqarah, Āli-'Imrān, an-Nisā', and al-Mā'idah or al-An'ām",[4] indicating that he prayed one of these *sūrahs* in each of the four *rak'ahs.*
- **Scholars' opinions**: According to the Ḥanafī, Shāfi'ī, and the Ḥanbalī schools, it is Sunnah to recite a *sūrah* or some passage from the Qur'ān in all the *rak'ahs* of the ṣalāh, whether it is two or four *rak'ah* long.[5]
- For more evidence on this, see *Qur'ān Recitation in the 3rd and the 4th Rak'ahs* on page 133 in the main book.

Reciting a Complete *Sūrah* in a *Rak'ah*

There are many ḥadīths that mention that the Prophet (s) recited a complete *sūrah* in a given *rak'ah.* These are cited in the section *Recitations of the Prophet (s) in Various Prayers* on page 59 below.

Reciting Multiple *Sūrahs* in a *Rak'ah*

- **He (s) recited multiple *sūrahs***: There are a number of ḥadīths that show that the Prophet (s) sometimes recited more than one *sūrah* in a particular *rak'ah*.

> 'Ā'isha (r) was asked, "Would the Messenger of Allāh (s) recite [more than one *sūrah*] in one *rak'ah*?" She replied, "[Yes, from the] *mufaṣṣal* (قالت: المفصل)." (Abū Dāwud)[6]

> Abū Wā'il narrated that a man came to Ibn Mas'ūd and said, "I recited all of the *mufaṣṣal*[3] in a single *rak'ah* last night." 'Abdullāh said, "This is like the hasty recitation of poetry ... I know the pairs that the Messenger of Allāh (s) used to put together", and he mentioned twenty *sūrahs* of the *mufaṣṣal*, two by two, in every *rak'ah* (سورتين سورتين في [كل] ركعة). (Muslim, Nasā'ī, Tirmidhī)[7]

- For more ḥadīths on this, see *Reciting Multiple Sūrahs in a Rak'ah* on page 134 in the main book.

Reciting Part of a *Sūrah* in a *Rak'ah*

- **He (s) recited part of a *sūrah***: One may also recite part of a *sūrah* in a *rak'ah*.

> 'Abdullāh ibn 'Abbās (r) narrated: "The Messenger of Allāh (s) used to recite in the two *rak'ahs* of Fajr *qūlū āmannā billāhi wa mā unzila ilainā* (*We believe in Allāh and what has been sent down to us*), the verse which is in al-Baqarah (2:136) in the first *rak'ah*, and in the second, *āmannā billāhi wa-sh-had bi-annanā muslimīn* (*We believe in Allāh and bear witness that we submit ourselves* (*to Him*)) (3:52)." (Muslim, Nasā'ī)[8]

---

[3] According to Ibn Kathīr, "Mufaṣṣal" *sūrahs* are those that begin from *sūrah* Qāf (*sūrah* 50) down to the last *sūrah* (an-Nās, *sūrah* 114). According to 'Abd al-Raḥmān al-Mubārakfūrī, the *musabbiḥāt sūrahs* are those that begin with *sabbiḥ* (glorify) or one of its forms. For more discussion on this, see *The Mufaṣṣal and Musabbiḥat Sūrahs* on page 507 in the main book.

> "It was narrated from ʿĀ'isha that the Messenger of Allāh (s) recited *sūrah* al-Aʿrāf in Maghrib and split it between two *rakʿahs* (فرقها في ركعتين)." (Nasā'ī)[9]

- For more ḥadīths on this, see *Reciting Part of a Sūrah in a Rakʿah* on page 135 in the main book.

Minimum Amount of Recitation

- **No textual reference**: There is no instruction recorded from the Messenger of Allāh (s) about what should be the minimum amount of recitation in ṣalāh. Some scholars set the minimum to three verses.

- **Unbroken expression**: Since there is no Prophetic instruction on this, what seems more important than setting an arbitrary limit is whether the recitation carries an unbroken expression. Sometimes, a single verse can be long but contain a full expression. On the other hand, a set of three verses may be incomplete in its expression. Therefore, the preferred opinion is that the minimum amount of recitation is not set to a fixed number of verses. If the verses are short, one should recite several verses and make sure that the expression is complete. However, if the verses are long, then one may recite less than three verses provided that the recitation carries an unbroken expression.

- **Definition, not recommendation**: This is only a legal definition of what may be considered to be the minimum required recitation, not that such minimum is recommended. Longer recitation in ṣalāh is more rewarding, especially when one is praying alone or making voluntary ṣalāh or when a long recitation by an *imām* would not cause any hardship on the followers.

- **Scholars' opinions**: According to the Ḥanbalī school, one must recite at least one verse that can stand independently. In other words, the recitation is acceptable if the sentence is complete without relying on the preceding or the following verse. So,

55:64 ("two gardens of the deepest green") and 74:21 ("and then he looks") is not acceptable since they cannot stand alone.[10]

- For a full discussion on this topic, see *Minimum Amount of Recitation* on page 129 in the main book. See also *Best Ṣalāh Is One with Long Recitation* on page 165 in the main book.

Recitation Is Shorter in the Subsequent *Rak'ahs*

- **Recommended practice**: When reciting from the Qur'ān after the *Fātiḥah*, it is recommended that recitation in a subsequent *rak'ah* be shorter than the recitation in the former *rak'ah*. This is evident from a number of ḥadīths.

> Abū Qatādah (r) narrated: "The Prophet (s) used to prolong the first *rak'ah* (يطول في الركعة الأولى) of the Ẓuhr ṣalāh and shorten the second (يقصر في الركعة الثانية) and he used to do the same in the morning ṣalāh." (Bukhārī, Muslim, Nasā'ī, Ibn Mājah)[11]

> Abū Salāmah (r) narrated: "The Messenger of Allāh (s) used to recite the *Ummu-l-Qur'ān* and two *sūrahs* in the first two *rak'ahs* of Ẓuhr and 'Aṣr and he would make us hear a verse sometimes, and he used to make the first *rak'ah* of Ẓuhr lengthy (يطول الركعة الأولى), and he did likewise in *Subḥ*." (Nasā'ī)[12]

- **Scholars' opinions**: According to all the schools of thought except the Mālikī, emulation of the Prophetic Sunnah is to make the 2nd *rak'ah* shorter than the first. The Ḥanafī and Shāfi'ī schools make an exception to this for the Friday prayers, the two 'Eīd prayers, and prayers in which large number of Muslims participate.[13] In the Mālikī school, it is "recommended" to make the 2nd *rak'ah* shorter.[14]

- For more ḥadīths on this, see *Recitation Is Shorter in the Subsequent Rak'ahs* on page 136 in the main book.

Recitation when Following an *Imām*

- **Recitation of the Fātiḥah**: When the *imām* is reciting the *Fātiḥah* loudly, then whether the followers should recite it (quietly) or not is a debatable issue among the scholars. As discussed above already (see *Reciting the Fātiḥah when Following an Imām* on page 48 above), the most sound opinion appears to be to listen to the *imām* when he recites the *Fātiḥah*.

- **Recitation of *sūrah***: When the *imām* is reciting *sūrah* (not the *Fātiḥah*) from the Qur'ān, then the followers should not recite anything but only listen. This is also the view of the Ḥanafī school.[15]

> Abū Hurairah (r) narrated: The Messenger of Allāh (s) said, "The *imām* has been appointed to be followed, so when he says *allāhu akbar*, then say *allāhu akbar*, when he recites, then listen attentively (وإذا قرأ فأنصتوا) ..." (Ibn Mājah, Nasā'ī)[16]

> Abū Mūsā al-Ashʿarī (r) narrated: The Messenger of Allāh (s) said, "When the *imām* recites, then listen attentively (إذا قرأ الإمام فأنصتوا) ..." (Ibn Mājah, Abū Dāwud)[17]

- For more evidence and a thorough discussion on this, see *Recitation when Following an Imām* on page 138 in the main book.

Recitations of the Prophet (s) in Various Prayers

- **His (s) usual practice**: According to the available ḥadīths in the *Six Most Authentic Books*, the Messenger of Allāh (s) recited the following *sūrahs* in the five obligatory and other prayers.

Ṣalāh	Recitation
sunnah of Fajr	2:136 (3 ½ lines) and 3:52 (2 ½ lines) 2:136 (3 ½ lines) and 3:64 (3 lines) 3:84 (3 ½ lines) and 3:52 (2 ½ lines) al-Kāfirūn (*sūrah* 109, ¼ page) and al-Ikhlāṣ (*sūrah* 112, ¼ page)

Fajr	al-Mu'minūn (*sūrah* 23, 8 pages) as-Sajdah (*sūrah* 32, 3 pages) and al-Insān (*sūrah* 76, 2 pages) Qāf (*sūrah* 50, 3 pages) al-Insān (*sūrah* 76, 2 pages) at-Takwīr (*sūrah* 81, 1 page) az-Zalzala (*sūrah* 99, ⅓ page) al-Falaq (*sūrah* 113, ¼ page) and an-Nās (*sūrah* 114, ¼ page) Long *mufaṣṣal sūrahs* In Fajr during Friday mornings, he (s) often used to recite *sūrah* as-Sajdah and *sūrah* al-Insān. One narration in Muslim specifically mentions that he would recite *sūrah* as-Sajdah in the first *rakʿah* and *sūrah* al-Insān in the second *rakʿah*.[18]
Ẓuhr	al-Burūj (*sūrah* 85, 1 page) and aṭ-Ṭāriq (*sūrah* 86, ½ page) al-Aʿlā (*sūrah* 87, ½ page) al-Lail (*sūrah* 92, ½ page) “30 verses”
ʿAṣr	al-Burūj (*sūrah* 85, 1 page) and aṭ-Ṭāriq (*sūrah* 86, ½ page) al-Aʿlā (*sūrah* 87, ½ page) al-Lail (*sūrah* 92, ½ page) Half of “30 verses”
Maghrib	al-Aʿrāf (*sūrah* 7, 26 pages) ad-Dukhān (*sūrah* 44, 3 pages) aṭ-Ṭūr (*sūrah* 44, 2 ½ pages) al-Mursalāt (*sūrah* 77, 1 ½ pages) Short *mufaṣṣal sūrahs*
ʿIshā'	al-Infiṭār (*sūrah* 82, ¾ page) al-Inshiqāq (*sūrah* 84, 1 page)

	al-Aʿlā (*sūrah* 87, ½ page) ash-Shams (*sūrah* 91, ½ page) al-Lail (*sūrah* 92, ½ page) aḍ-Ḍuḥā (*sūrah* 93, ⅓ page) at-Tīn (*sūrah* 95, ⅓ page) al-ʿAlaq (*sūrah* 96, ½ page) Medium *mufaṣṣal sūrahs*
Jumuʿah	al-Jumuʿah (*sūrah* 62, 1 ½ page) and al-Munāfiqūn (*sūrah* 63, 1 ½ page) al-Aʿlā (*sūrah* 87, ½ page) and al-Ghāshiyah (*sūrah* 88, ¾ page)
Witr	al-Aʿlā (*sūrah* 87, ½ page), al-Kāfirūn (*sūrah* 209, ¼ page), and al-Ikhlāṣ (*sūrah* 112, ¼ page)
ʿEīd	Qāf (*sūrah* 50, 3 pages) and al-Qamar (*sūrah* 54, 2 ½ page) al-Aʿlā (*sūrah* 87, ½ page) and al-Ghāshiyah (*sūrah* 88, ¾ page)
Tahajjud	al-Baqarah (*sūrah* 2, 48 pages) Āli-ʿImrān (*sūrah* 3, 27 pages) an-Nisā' (*sūrah* 4, 29 ½ pages) al-Mā'idah (*sūrah* 5, 21 ½ pages) al-Anʿām (*sūrah* 6, 23 pages)
Ṭawāf	aṭ-Ṭūr (*sūrah* 52, 2 ½ pages) al-Kāfirūn (*sūrah* 109, ¼ page) al-Ikhlāṣ (*sūrah* 112, ¼ page)

- For supporting ḥadīths on the above, see *Recitations of the Prophet (s) in Various Prayers* on page 144 in the main book.

Virtues of Specific *Sūrahs* and Verses

- ***Sūrah*/verse list**: Besides the above *sūrahs* that the Messenger of Allāh (s) recited in various prayers, there are a number of *sūrahs* and verses that he (s) described as virtuous. It will, therefore, be recommended to recite them often.

Sūrah	Virtues
1: al-Fātiḥah (1 page)	• One of the "two lights" that were given to the Prophet (s) and not to any other Prophet. "You will never recite one letter of them (لن تقرأ بحرف منهما) but you will be given reward (إلا أعطيته)." (Muslim, Nasā'ī)[19] • Ḥadīth *qudsī*: "I have divided the ṣalāh (i.e., the Fātiḥah) between Myself and My slaves into two halves. Half of it is for Me, and half of it is for My slave, and My slave will have what he asks for (ولعبدي ما سأل) ..." (Tirmidhī)[20] • It is "the greatest *sūrah* in the Qur'ān (أعظم سورة في القرآن)." (Bukhārī, Nasā'ī, Abū Dāwud)[21] • "the like of it (al-Fātiḥah) has never been revealed (ما أنزلت ... مثلها) in the *Tawrah* nor the *Injīl* nor the *Zabūr* nor in the *Furqān*." (Tirmidhī)[22]
2: al-Baqarah (48 pages)	• "Shaiṭān flees from a house (إن الشيطان ينفر من البيت) in which *sūrah* al-Baqarah is recited." (Muslim)[23] • One of the "two bright ones" that will come on the Day of Resurrection "pleading on behalf of their companions (تحاجان عن أصحابهما)" and that the magicians "cannot withstand it." (Muslim)[24]
2:255 *Ayātu-l-Kursī* (⅓ page)	• The "greatest" verse in the Qur'ān. (Muslim, Abū Dāwud)[25] • If one recites it when going to bed, "Allāh will appoint a guard for you who will stay with you

	and no Shaiṭān will come near you till the morning." (Bukhārī)[26]
2:285-86 (½ page)	• One of the "two lights" that were given to the Prophet (s) and not to any other Prophet. "You will never recite one letter of them but you will be given reward (لن تقرأ بحرف منهما إلا أعطيته)." (Muslim, Nasā'ī)[27] • Anyone who recites them at night, "that will be sufficient for him (كفتاه)." (Bukhārī, Muslim, Abū Dāwud, Ibn Mājah, Tirmidhī)[28] • "If they are recited for three nights in a home, no Shaiṭān will come near it." (Tirmidhī)[29]*
3: Āli-ʿImrān (27 pages)	• One of the "two bright ones" that will come on the Day of Resurrection "pleading on behalf of their companions (تحاجان عن أصحابهما)" and that the magicians "cannot withstand it." (Muslim)[30]
18: al-Kahf (11 pages)	• A man was reciting *sūrah* al-Kahf, because of which "a cloud overshadowed" his house and "tranquility came down." (Muslim)[31]
18: al-Kahf first or last 10 verses (¾ page) or, first three verses	• "Whoever memorizes ten verses from the beginning of *sūrah* al-Kahf, will be protected from the tribulation of the Dajjāl (عُصم من فتنة الدّجّال)." (Muslim)[32] • "whoever recites three *āyahs* from the beginning of al-Kahf, he is protected from the turmoil of the Dajjāl." (Tirmidhī)[33]
67: al-Mulk (2 ½ pages)	• "It will intercede on behalf of its companions until he is forgiven (تشفع لصاحبها حتى غفر له)." (Abū Dāwud, Tirmidhī)[34]*

109: al-Kāfirūn (¼ page)	• He (s) advised a man to recite when going to bed, for "verily it is a disavowal of shirk (فإنها براءة من الشرك)." (Tirmidhī)[35]*
112: al-Ikhlāṣ (¼ page)	• It is equivalent to "one-third of the Qur'ān (ثلث القرآن)" (Bukhari, Muslim, Tirmidhī, Nasa'i, Abū Dāwud, Ibn Majah)[36] • A man was reciting it. The Messenger of Allāh (s) said, "It is guaranteed (وجبت)." He was asked, "What, O Messenger of Allāh (swt)?" He said, "Paradise (الجنة)." (Nasā'ī, Tirmidhī)[37]* • A man used to lead others in ṣalāh and end his recitation with this *sūrah* "because it is a description of the Most Merciful and I love to recite it." The Prophet (s) said, "Tell him that Allāh loves him (أخبروه أن الله يحبه)." (Muslim)[38] • Before going to bed each night, the Prophet (s) would recite *sūrahs* al-Ikhlāṣ, al-Falaq, and an-Nās, blow in his hands, and wipe his head, face, and front part of his body with them three times. (Bukhārī, Abū Dāwud)[39] • A man used to lead ṣalāh and recite *qul huwa allāhu aḥad* followed by another *sūrah* in every *rak'ah*. When asked by the Prophet (s) as to why, he said, "O Messenger of Allāh (s)! I indeed love it." He (s) said, "Your love for it shall have you admitted into Paradise (إن حبها أدخلك الجنة)." (Tirmidhī)[40] • He (s) said, "No one ever sought refuge by means of anything like them", i.e., *sūrahs* al-Ikhlāṣ, al-Falaq, and an-Nās. (Nasā'ī)[41]* • Reciting *sūrahs* al-Ikhlāṣ, al-Falaq, and an-Nās every evening and morning "will suffice you against everything (تكفيك من كل شيء)." (Tirmidhī, Nasā'ī)[42]*

113: al-Falaq (¼ page) 114: an-Nās (¼ page)	• When *sūrahs* al-Falaq and an-Nās were revealed, the Prophet (s) said that the like of them "has never been seen (لم ير مثلهن قط)." (Muslim, Nasā'ī, Tirmidhī)[43] • He (s) told ʿUqbah bin ʿĀmīr (r), "You will never recite anything greater before Allāh (لن تقرأ شيئا أبلغ عند الله) than *qul aʿūdhu bi rabbi-l-falaq* (*sūrah* 113) and *qul aʿūdhu bi rabbi-n-nās* (*sūrah* 114)." (Nasā'ī)[44] • He (s) said that al-Falaq and an-Nās are "two of the best *sūrahs*." (Nasā'ī)[45] • Before going to bed each night, the Prophet (s) would recite *sūrahs* al-Ikhlāṣ, al-Falaq, and an-Nās, blow in his hands, and wipe his head, face, and front part of his body with them three times. (Bukhārī, Abū Dāwud)[46] • The Prophet (s) told Jābir bin ʿAbdullāh (r) to recite al-Falaq and an-Nās, "for you will never recite anything like them (اقرأ بهما ولن تقرأ بمثلهما)." (Nasā'ī)[47]* • He (s) said, "No one ever sought refuge by means of anything like them", i.e., *sūrahs* al-Ikhlāṣ, al-Falaq, and an-Nās. (Nasā'ī)[48]* • Reciting *sūrahs* al-Ikhlāṣ, al-Falaq, and an-Nās every evening and morning "will suffice you against everything (تكفيك من كل شيء)." (Tirmidhī, Nasā'ī)[49]* • "People cannot seek refuge with Allāh by means of anything better than these two (ما تعوذ الناس بأفضل منهما)." (i.e., *sūrahs* al-Falaq and an-Nās) (Nasā'ī)[50]*

* Graded *ḥasan*

- For all the ḥadīths associated with these reports, see *Virtues of Specific Sūrahs and Verses* on page 169 in the main book.

Order of Recitation

- **No prohibitive text**: The *Six Most Authentic Books* do not contain any ḥadīth that prohibits non-sequential recitation. However, there are more ḥadīths available that show that the Prophet (s) recited based on the sequential order of *sūrahs* than where the recitations were non-sequential. For example:

> ʿAbdullāh ibn ʿAbbās (r) narrated: "The Messenger of Allāh (s) used to recite in the two *rakʿahs* of Fajr: in the first *rakʿah, qūlū āmannā billāhi wa mā unzila ilainā* (*We believe in Allāh and what has been sent down to us*), the verse which is in al-Baqarah (2:136), and in the second, *āmannā billāhi wa-sh-had bi annanā muslimīn* (*We believe in Allāh and bear witness that we submit ourselves* (*to Him*)) (3:52)." (Muslim, Nasāʾī)[51]

> Ubay bin Kaʿb (r) narrated: "In the first *rakʿah* of Witr, the Messenger of Allāh (s) used to recite *sabbiḥi-isma rabbika-l-aʿlā* (*Glorify the Name of your Lord, the Most High*) (*sūrah* 87), in the second *qul yā ayyuha-l-kāfirūn* (*Say: O you disbelievers!*) (*sūrah* 109), and in the third *qul huwa allāhu aḥad* (*Say: He is Allāh, the One*) (*sūrah* 112)." (Nasāʾī, Abū Dāwud, Ibn Mājah)[52]

- **Recommendation only**: Based on the above, and from the fact that an out-of-order recitation can break up the meaning, it would be recommended that one maintains the sequential order of the *sūrahs* or the verses.

- **Scholars' opinions**: According to all the four schools, it is *makruh* (disliked) to recite without maintaining the sequential order.[53]

- For more evidence and a detailed discussion on this, see *Order of Recitation* on page 181 in the main book.

Beautifying the Recitation

- **Proper etiquette**: Qur'ān is the Book of Allāh (swt). It requires proper etiquette when one recites it. This includes:
    - Understanding what is being recited.
    - Reciting with a measured pace without haste.
    - Following proper rules of recitation (*tajwīd*) or making efforts to do so, and
    - Beautifying the recitation (*tartīl*).

> Abū Hurairah (r) narrated: The Messenger of Allāh (s) said, "If one of you gets up to pray at night and falters in his recitation of the Qur'ān (فاستعجم القرآن على لسانه), and does not know what he is saying (لم يدر ما يقول), let him lie down." (Muslim, Ibn Mājah)[54]

> [Paraphrasing: Ḥudhaifah narrated that he once prayed nightly ṣalāh behind the Prophet (s) in which] "... he started to recite Āli-ʿImrān and recited it all, reciting with a slow and measured pace (يقرأ مترسلا). When he reached a verse that spoke of glorifying Allāh, he glorified Allāh; when he reached a verse that spoke of asking Him, he asked of Him; when he reached a verse that spoke of seeking refuge with Him, he sought refuge with Him ..." (Muslim)[55]

> ʿĀ'isha (r) narrated: The Messenger of Allāh (s) said, "The one who is skilled in reciting the Qur'ān (الماهر بالقرآن) will be with the noble, honorable scribes and the one who recites the Qur'ān and falters therein, and finds it difficult, will have a double reward." (Muslim, Tirmidhī, Ibn Mājah)[56]

> Al-Barā' bin ʿĀzib (r) narrated: "I heard the Prophet (s) reciting *wa-t-tini wa-z-zaitūni* in the ʿIshā' ṣalāh, and I never heard a more beautiful voice or a better recitation than that of him (أحسن صوتا منه أو قراءة)." (Bukhārī, Muslim, Ibn Mājah)[57]

- **Scholars' opinions**: In the Ḥanbalī school, emulation of the Prophetic example is to recite the Qur'ān in a melodious voice.[58]

- For more evidence and discussion on this topic, see *Beautifying the Recitation* on page 184 in the main book.

Best Ṣalāh Is One with Long Recitation

- **When praying alone**: It is preferable to make the recitation long, especially when one is praying alone. The Messenger of Allāh (s) said that long recitation makes the ṣalāh best.

> Jābir bin ʿAbdullāh (r) narrated: The Messenger of Allāh (s) said, "The best ṣalāh is that in which one stands for a long time (أفضل الصلاة طول القنوت)." (Muslim, Ibn Mājah, Tirmidhī)[59]

- For more evidence on this, see *Best Ṣalāh Is One with Long Recitation* on page 165 in the main book.

Consideration for the Weak, the Old, and the Children

- **Making short recitations when leading**: Longer recitation is meritorious only when one is praying alone or when the congregation does not have weak, sick, old, or young people in it, or people with urgent needs.

> Abū Hurairah (r) narrated: The Messenger of Allāh (s) said, "If anyone of you leads the people in ṣalāh, let him shorten it (فَلْيُخَفِّفْ), for among them are the weak (الضَّعِيفَ), the sick (وَالسَّقِيمَ), and the old (وَالكَبِيرَ); and if anyone among you offers ṣalāh alone, then he may prolong as much as he wishes." (Bukhārī, Muslim, Nasā'ī, Abū Dāwud, Tirmidhī)[60]

> Anas bin Mālik (r) narrated: "I never offered a ṣalāh behind any *imām* that is lighter and more perfect than one behind the Prophet (s). Whenever he heard the cries of a child, he used to cut it short fearing that his mother would be tormented (فَيُخَفِّفُ مَخَافَةَ أَنْ تُفْتَنَ أُمُّهُ)." (Bukhārī, Tirmidhī)[61]

- **Scholars' opinions**: According to the Ḥanbalī school, the Prophetic example is not to prolong recitation when leading others.[62]

The Mālikī and Shāfiʿī schools hold that the Sunnah is to prolong recitation when one leads a small group and they give their consent for long recitation. According to the Ḥanafī school, it is Sunnah for the *imām* to prolong recitation only if he knows that it will pose no hardship for the followers.[63]

- For more evidence/discussion on this, see *Consideration for the Weak, the Old, and the Children* on page 189 in the main book.

Audible and Quiet Prayers

- **Audible prayers**: In Fajr and in the first two *rakʿahs* of Maghrib and ʿIshā' prayers, the Messenger of Allāh (s) used to make his recitation loud. There are many ḥadīths that mention that the Companions (r) heard the Messenger of Allāh (s) reciting entire *sūrahs* or part of a *sūrah* in Fajr, Maghrib, and ʿIshā' prayers.

> ʿAmr bin Ḥuraith (r) narrated: "I heard the Prophet (s) reciting *idha-sh-shamsu kuwwirat* (*When the sun is overthrown*) (*sūrah* 81) in Fajr." (Nasā'ī, Muslim, Abū Dāwud, Ibn Mājah)[64]

> Jubair bin Muṭʿim (r) narrated: "I heard Allāh's Messenger (s) reciting at-Ṭūr (*sūrah* 52) in Maghrib." (Bukhārī, Muslim, Nasā'ī, Abū Dāwud, Tirmidhī)[65]

> Al-Barā' bin ʿĀzib (r) narrated: "The Prophet (s) was on journey and recited in one of the first two *rakʿahs* of the ʿIshā' ṣalāh *wa-t-tīni wa-z-zaitūni* (*By the Fig and the Olive*) (*sūrah* 95)." (Bukhārī, Muslim, Nasā'ī, Abū Dāwud)[66]

- **Quiet prayers**: In Ẓuhr and ʿAṣr prayers, he (s) would recite quietly.

> Abū Qatādah (r) narrated: "The Prophet (s) used to recite *sūrah* al-Fātiḥah along with another *sūrah* in the first two *rakʿahs* of Ẓuhr and ʿAṣr prayers, and he would make us hear a verse sometimes (ويسمعنا الآية أحيانا)." (Bukhārī, Muslim, Abū Dāwud, Ibn Mājah, Nasā'ī)[67]

- **Scholars' opinions**: According to all the four schools, emulation of the Prophetic Sunnah is to recite audibly in the Fajr ṣalāh, the first two *rak'ahs* of Maghrib and 'Ishā' prayers, the Jumu'ah ṣalāh, and the two 'Eīd prayers. As for the rest of the daily prayers, the Prophetic example is to recite quietly in them according to Ḥanafī, Shāfi'ī and the Ḥanbalī schools.[68]

- For more evidence, see *Audible and Quiet Prayers* on page 166 in the main book.

Tongue Must Be Moved During Quiet Recitations

- **Not reciting "in mind"**: When recitation is done quietly, it is not sufficient to recite "in mind"; one must also move the tongue and recite in a soft voice so that he can hear it himself.

- **His (s) beard would move**: When the Companions prayed behind the Messenger of Allāh (s) during Ẓuhr and 'Aṣr prayers in which he recited quietly, they would know that he was reciting "from the movement of his beard." It is also reported that during recitations in Ẓuhr and 'Aṣr prayers, "he would make us hear a verse sometimes." The ḥadīth of Abū Qatādah (r) on this has already been cited above.

> "We asked Khabbāb (r) whether Allāh's Messenger (s) used to recite in the Ẓuhr and the 'Aṣr prayers. He replied in the affirmative. We said, 'How did you come to know about it?' He said, 'From the movement of his beard' (باضطراب لحيته)." (Bukhārī, Abū Dāwud, Ibn Mājah)[69]

- **Scholars' opinions**: All the schools except the Mālikī agree that emulation of the Prophetic Sunnah, when reciting in the quiet prayers, is to recite in a low voice so that one can hear himself. Even in the Mālikī school, it is "recommended" to do so.[70]

- For more evidence on this, see *Tongue Must Be Moved During Quiet Recitations* on page 168 in the main book.

---

[1] Muslim, *Ṣalāh*, 1013; Nasā'ī, *Commencement of Ṣalāh*, 978.

[2] Nasā'ī, *Commencement of Ṣalāh*, 979.

[3] Al-Jazīrī, *Islamic Jurisprudence*, p. 330.

[4] Abū Dāwud, *Ṣalāh*, 874.

[5] Al-Jazīrī, *Islamic Jurisprudence*, pp. 330-31.

[6] Abū Dāwud, *Ṣalāh*, 956; *Voluntary Prayers*, 1292.

[7] Muslim, *Virtues of the Qur'ān*, 1913, 1912, Nasā'ī, *Commencement of Ṣalāh*, 1006, 1005, 1007; Tirmidhī, *Traveling*, 602.

[8] Muslim, *Traveller's Prayer*, 1691; Nasā'ī, *Commencement of Ṣalāh*, 945.

[9] Nasā'ī, *Commencement of Ṣalāh*, 992.

[10] Al-Jazīrī, *Islamic Jurisprudence*, p. 330. Majority of the Shāfi'ī scholars consider three verses to be the minimum but a longer verse is preferable than three short verses. According to the Ḥanafī school, the minimum amount of recitation is three short verses or one long verse that equals three short verses. In the Mālikī school, a small *sūrah*, a verse, or event part of a verse would fulfill the *sunnah*. (See Al-Jazīrī, *Islamic Jurisprudence*, pp. 299, 320, 330.)

[11] Bukhārī, *Adhān*, 779; Muslim, *Ṣalāh*, 1012; Nasā'ī, *Commencement of Ṣalāh*, 975; Ibn Mājah, *Establishing Ṣalāh*, 819.

[12] Nasā'ī, *Commencement of Ṣalāh*, 979.

[13] Al-Jazīrī, *Islamic Jurisprudence*, pp. 320, 323, 336.

[14] *Ibid.*, p. 336.

[15] *Ibid.*, p. 330.

[16] Ibn Mājah, *Establishing Ṣalāh*, 846; Nasā'ī, *Commencement of Ṣalāh*, 923.

[17] Ibn Mājah, *Establishing Ṣalāh*, 847; Abū Dāwud, *Ṣalāh*, 973.

[18] Muslim, *Jumu'ah*, 2035.

[19] Muslim, *Virtues of the Qur'ān*, 1877; Nasā'ī, *Commencement of Ṣalāh*, 913.

[20] Tirmidhī, *Tafsīr*, 2953.

[21] Bukhārī, *Virtues of the Qur'ān*, 5006; Nasā'ī, *Commencement of Ṣalāh*, 914; Abū Dāwud, *Witr*, 1458.

[22] Tirmidhī, *Virtues of the Qur'ān*, 2875.

[23] Muslim, *Traveller's Prayer*, 1824.

[24] Muslim, *Virtues of the Qur'ān*, 1874-75.

[25] Muslim, *Virtues of the Qur'ān*, 1885; Abū Dāwud, *Witr*, 1460.

[26] Bukhārī, *Representation*, 2311; *Virtues of the Qur'ān*, 5010.

[27] Muslim, *Virtues of the Qur'ān*, 1877; Nasā'ī, *Commencement of Ṣalāh*, 913.

[28] Bukhārī, *Virtues of the Qur'ān*, 5008-09, 5040; Muslim, *Virtues of the Qur'ān*, 1878-82; Abū Dāwud, *Month of Ramaḍān*, 1397; Ibn Mājah, *Establishing Ṣalāh*, 1368-69; Tirmidhī, *Virtues of the Qur'ān*, 2881.

[29] Tirmidhī, *Virtues of the Qur'ān*, 2882, graded *ḥasan*.

[30] Muslim, *Virtues of the Qur'ān*, 1874-75.

[31] Muslim, *Virtues of the Qur'ān*, 1856-58.

[32] Muslim, *Virtues of the Qur'ān*, 1883.

[33] Tirmidhī, *Virtues of the Qur'ān*, 2886.

[34] Abū Dāwud, *Month of Ramaḍān*, 1400; Tirmidhī, *Virtues of the Qur'ān*, 2891; both graded *ḥasan*.

[35] Tirmidhī, *Supplications*, 3403, graded *ḥasan*.

[36] Bukhārī, *Virtues of the Qur'ān*, 5013; Muslim, *Virtues of the Qur'ān*, 1889, 1887-88; Tirmidhī, *Virtues of the Qur'ān*, 2900; Nasā'ī, *Commencement of Ṣalāh*, 996; Abū Dāwud, *Witr*, 1461; Ibn Mājah, *Etiquette*, 3787.

[37] Nasā'ī, *Commencement of Ṣalāh*, 995; Tirmidhī, *Virtues of the Qur'ān*, 2897; both graded ḥasan.

[38] Muslim, *Virtues of the Qur'ān*, 1890.

[39] Bukhārī, *Virtues of the Qur'ān*, 5017; Abū Dāwud, *Etiquette*, 5056.

[40] Tirmidhī, *Virtues of the Qur'ān*, 2901.

[41] Nasā'ī, *Seeking Refuge*, 5432-33, 5435, 5439; all graded *ḥasan*. Narration 5435 only mentions *sūrah* 113, while narration 5439 only mentions *sūrah* 113 and 114.

[42] Tirmidhī, *Narrations On Supplications*, 3575; Nasā'ī, *Seeking Refuge*, 5430; both graded *ḥasan*.

[43] Muslim, *Virtues of the Qur'ān*, 1891-93; Nasā'ī, *Commencement of Ṣalāh*, 955; *Seeking Refuge*, 5442; Tirmidhī, *Virtues of the Qur'ān*, 2902.

[44] Nasā'ī, *Commencement of Ṣalāh*, 954; *Seeking Refuge*, 5441. Narration 5441 only mentions *sūrah* 113.

[45] Nasā'ī, *Seeking Refuge*, 5439.

[46] Bukhārī, *Virtues of the Qur'ān*, 5017; Abū Dāwud, *Etiquette*, 5056

[47] Nasā'ī, *Seeking Refuge*, 5443, graded *ḥasan*.

[48] Nasā'ī, *Seeking Refuge*, 5432-33, 5435, 5439; all graded *ḥasan*. Narration 5435 only mentions *sūrah* 113 and nar. 5439 only mentions *sūrah* 113 and 114.

[49] Tirmidhī, *Narrations On Supplications*, 3575; Nasā'ī, *Seeking Refuge*, 5430; both graded *ḥasan*.

---

[50] Nasā'ī, *Seeking Refuge*, 5431, graded *ḥasan*.

[51] Muslim, *Traveller's Prayer*, 1691; Nasā'ī, *Commencement of Ṣalāh*, 945.

[52] Nasā'ī, *Qiyām al-Lail*, 1700-01, 1730-31; Abū Dāwud, *Witr*, 1423; Ibn Mājah, *Establishing Ṣalāh*, 1171.

[53] Al-Zuhayly, *Al-Fiqh al-Islami wa Adillatuh*, vol. 1, p. 699.

[54] Muslim, *Traveller's Prayer*, 1836; Ibn Mājah, *Establishing Ṣalāh*, 1372.

[55] Muslim, *Traveller's Prayer*, 1814.

[56] Muslim, *Virtues of the Qur'ān*, 1862; Tirmidhī, *Virtues of the Qur'ān*, 2904; Ibn Mājah, *Etiquette*, 3779.

[57] Bukhārī, *Adhān*, 769; *Tauḥīd*, 7546; Muslim, *Ṣalāh*, 1039; Ibn Mājah, *Establishing Ṣalāh*, 835.

[58] Al-Jazīrī, *Islamic Jurisprudence*, p. 323.

[59] Muslim, *Traveller's Prayer*, 1768-69; Ibn Mājah, *Establishing Ṣalāh*, 1421; Tirmidhī, *Ṣalāh*, 387.

[60] Bukhārī, *Adhān*, 703; Muslim, *Ṣalāh*, 1046-47; Nasā'ī, *Leading Ṣalāh*, 824; Abū Dāwud, *Ṣalāh*, 794; Tirmidhī, *Ṣalāh*, 236.

[61] Bukhārī, *Adhān*, 708; Tirmidhī, *Ṣalāh*, 376.

[62] Al-Jazīrī, *Islamic Jurisprudence*, p. 232.

[63] *Ibid.*, pp. 335-36.

[64] Nasā'ī, *Commencement of Ṣalāh*, 952; Muslim, *Ṣalāh*, 1023, 1066; Abū Dāwud, *Ṣalāh*, 817; Ibn Mājah, *Establishing Ṣalāh*, 817.

[65] Bukhārī, *Adhān*, 765; *Commentary*, 4854; Muslim, *Ṣalāh*, 1035-36; Nasā'ī, *Commencement of Ṣalāh*, 988; Abū Dāwud, *Ṣalāh*, 811; Ibn Mājah, *Establishing Ṣalāh*, 832.

[66] Bukhārī, *Adhān*, 767; *Commentary*, 4952; Muslim, *Ṣalāh*, 1037; Nasā'ī, *Commencement of Ṣalāh*, 1002; Abū Dāwud, *Traveler's Prayer*, 1221.

[67] Bukhārī, *Adhān*, 762, 759, 776, 778; Muslim, *Ṣalāh*, 1012-13; Abū Dāwud, *Ṣalāh*, 798-800; Ibn Mājah, *Establishing Ṣalāh*, 829; Nasā'ī, *Commencement of Ṣalāh*, 976-79.

[68] Al-Jazīrī, *Islamic Jurisprudence*, pp. 339-40.

[69] Bukhārī, *Adhān*, 746, 760-61, 777; Abū Dāwud, *Ṣalāh*, 801; Ibn Mājah, *Establishing Ṣalāh*, 826.

[70] Al-Jazīrī, *Islamic Jurisprudence*, pp. 319, 341, 347. The Ḥanafī school goes further and states that a nearby person should also be able to hear one's "silent" recitation. (*Ibid.*, p. 341.)

The *Rukū*‘ (الركوع)

After completing his recitation, the Messenger of Allāh (s) would go to the *rukū*‘.

Saying the *Takbīr* Before Going to *Rukū*‘

- ***Takbīr* before *rukū*‘**: Before going to the *rukū*‘, the Messenger of Allāh (s) would say the *takbīr*.

> ‘Abdullāh ibn ‘Umar (r) narrated: “The Messenger of Allāh (s) used to raise both his hands up to the level of his shoulders when opening ṣalāh and on saying the *takbīr* for *rukū*‘ (وإذا كبّر للركوع) ...” (Bukhārī, Muslim, Abū Dāwud, Ibn Mājah, Nasā'ī, Tirmidhī)[1]

- For more evidence on this, see *Ḥadīths on Takbīr when Going into Rukū*‘ on page 204 in the main book.

Raising the Hands Before Going to *Rukū*‘

- **Many ḥadīths on raising the hands**: The Messenger of Allāh (s) used to raise his hands before he went to the *rukū*‘ and after he stood up from the *rukū*‘. The ḥadīth about this *Raf*‘ *al-Yadain* (raising the hands during *rukū*‘) is considered *mutawātir* by ḥadīth scholars.[2] Multiple companions narrated ḥadīths about this. Mentioned below are a few among them.

> ‘Abdullāh ibn ‘Umar (r) narrated: “The Messenger of Allāh (s) used to raise both his hands (كان يرفع يديه) up to the level of his shoulders when opening ṣalāh and on saying the *takbīr* for making *rukū*‘

(وإذا كبّر للركوع), and on raising up his head from the *rukū*ʿ (وإذا رفع رأسه من الركوع) he would do likewise raise them also (رفعهما كذلك أيضا) ..." (Bukhārī, Muslim, Abū Dāwud, Ibn Mājah, Nasā'ī, Tirmidhī)[3]

Wā'il bin Ḥujr (r) narrated: "... When he (s) wanted to make *rukū*ʿ (فلما أراد أن يركع), he brought his hands out from his garment and raised them (ثم رفعهما), then he said the *takbīr* and made *rukū*ʿ. When he said *sami*ʿ *allāhu liman ḥamidah*, he raised his hands (رفع يديه) ..." (Muslim, Abū Dāwud, Ibn Mājah, Nasā'ī)[4]

Anas bin Mālik (r) narrated: "The Messenger of Allāh (s) used to raise his hands (كان يرفع يديه) when he entered ṣalāh, and when he made *rukū*ʿ (وإذا ركع)." (Ibn Mājah)[5]

Abū Hurairah (r) narrated: [When the Messenger of Allāh (s)] "said the *takbīr* for the ṣalāh, he would raise his hands (جعل يديه) ... and when he went to *rukū*ʿ (وإذا ركع) he would do the same (فعل مثل ذلك), and when he raised himself (after *rukū*ʿ) to go into *sujūd* (وإذا رفع للسجود), he would do the same, and when he raised himself after two *rak*ʿ*ahs*, he would do the same." (Abū Dāwud)[6]

- **No *ṣaḥīḥ* ḥadīths against it**: The *Six Most Authentic Books* do not contain any *ṣaḥīḥ* or *ḥasan* ḥadīth against raising the hands before or after the *rukū*ʿ.
- **Scholars' opinions**: According to the Shāfiʿī and the Ḥanbalī schools, it is from the Prophetic example to raise the hands before one goes to the *rukū*ʿ and after he stands up from the *rukū*ʿ.[7]
- **Supported by most scholars of ḥadīth and *fiqh***: Majority of the scholars of ḥadīth and *fiqh* support *Raf*ʿ *al-Yadain*, including some Ḥanafī scholars.[8]

- For a complete list of ḥadīths on this subject and a detailed discussion, see *Raising the Hands Before/After Rukū'* on page 209 in the main book.

Arguments Against Raising the Hands Before Going to *Rukū'*

According to the Ḥanafī school, hands should not be raised before/after the *rukū'*. The major arguments in support of this view have been fully addressed in the section *Arguments Against Raf' al-Yadain* on page 216 in the main book.

Manner of Performing *Rukū'*

Making *rukū'* properly according to the example of the Messenger of Allāh (s) involves a number of elements. These are described below.

Hands on the Knees

- **Where to place the hands**: When the Prophet (s) made *rukū'*, he would place his hands on his knees.

> Abū Ḥumaid as-Sā'idī (r) narrated: "When the Prophet (s) made *rukū'* ... he placed his hands on his knees (ووضع يديه على ركبتيه)." (Nasā'ī, Abū Dāwud, Tirmidhī)[9]

> Sa'd bin Abī Waqqāṣ (r) narrated: "... We ... were ordered (أُمرنا) to place the hands on the knees (أن نضع أيدينا على الركب)." (Bukhārī, Muslim, Abū Dāwud)[10]

- For more evidence on this, see *Hands on the Knees* on page 235 in the main book.

Hands and Knees Should Support the Weight of the Body

The hands should not merely touch the knees; they need to also support the full weight of the back.

> Abū Ḥumaid as-Sā'idī (r) narrated: [The Prophet (s) would go to *rukū'*] "... placing his palms on his knees and supporting his weight on them (ويضع راحتيه على ركبتيه معتمدا) ..." (Ibn Mājah)[11]

Grasping the Knees, Fingers Spaced out Below the Knees

- **Firmly holding the knees**: The Messenger of Allāh (s) would also grasp his knees firmly, and not merely touch them.

> [Describing the ṣalāh of the Prophet (s), Abū Ḥumaid as-Sā'idī said:] "… on making *rukū'*, he grasped his knees with his hands (أمكن يديه من ركبتيه) and bent his back straight ..." (Bukhārī)[12]

- **Scholars' opinions**: According to the Mālikī school, it is recommended to place the hands firmly on the knees and keep the knees and the back straight. Keeping the fingers close or apart is up to the individual as long as he holds on to the knees firmly.[13] According to the Ḥanafī and Ḥanbalī schools, the Prophetic example is to place the hands on knees and spread the fingers.[14]

- For additional ḥadīths on this, see *Grasping the Knees, Fingers Spaced out Below the Knees* on page 237 in the main book.

Arms Should Be Away from the Sides

- **He (s) kept his arms away from the sides**: There are some narrations that show that when the Messenger of Allāh (s) went to the *rukū'*, he would keep his arms away from his sides.

> [Abū Ḥumaid as-Sā'idī (r) demonstrated the ṣalāh of the Prophet (s):] "... then he went into *rukū'* and placed his hands on his knees as if he were grabbing them and he bent his hands (arms) such that they were away from his sides (ووتر يديه فتجافى عن جنبيه) ..." (Abū Dāwud)[15]

- **Scholars' opinions**: According to the Ḥanbalī school, the Sunnah is to keep the upper arms away from the sides when in *rukū'*.[16] The Mālikī school also holds that it is "recommended" to keep the elbows/upper arms away from the sides during the *rukū'*.[17]

- For additional ḥadīths on this, see *Arms Should Be Away from the Sides* on page 239 in the main book.

Back and Head to Be Kept Straight

- **Back kept even**: When the Messenger of Allāh (s) went to the *rukū*ʿ, he kept his back even and balanced.

> Abū Ḥumaid as-Sāʿidī (r) narrated: "When the Prophet (s) made *rukū*ʿ, he was balanced (اعتدل); he would neither lower his back, nor raise it up (فلم ينصب رأسه ولم يقنعه)." (Nasāʾī, Ibn Mājah, Abū Dāwud, Tirmidhī)[18]

> [Describing the ṣalāh of the Prophet (s), Abū Ḥumaid as-Sāʿidī said:] "... on making *rukū*ʿ, he grasped his knees with his hands and bent his back straight (ثُمَّ هَصَرَ ظَهْرَهُ) ..." (Bukhārī)[19]

- **Head and neck straight**: He (s) also kept his head and neck straight.

> ʿĀ'isha (r) narrated: "The Messenger of Allāh (s) ... when he made *rukū*ʿ, he neither kept his head up (لم يشخص رأسه) nor lowered it (ولم يصوبه), but it was somewhere between the two (ولكن بين ذلك) ..." (Muslim, Abū Dāwud, Ibn Mājah)[20]

- **Scholars' opinions**: According to the Ḥanafī school, one should bend at the hip so that the back and the legs are straight and the head is in the same level with the buttocks. In the Ḥanbalī school, the back should be parallel to the ground and the head should be at the same level as the back. According to the Shāfiʿī school, one should bend deep enough so that the head and the back are in a straight line.[21]

- For more evidence on this topic, see *Back and Head to Be Kept Straight* on page 240 in the main book.

Where to Look when in *Rukū*ʿ

- **No textual reference**: The *Six Most Authentic Books* do not contain any ḥadīth that explicitly mentions whether one should be looking at the place of the *sajdah*, straight down, or near the feet while in *rukū*ʿ.

- **Emphasis on keeping the back straight**: All these options are perhaps valid as long as one keeps his head at the same level as the back of his body without tilting his head up or down. If looking at the feet makes the head tilt downwards, or looking at the place of the *sajdah* makes it tilt upwards, then one should look straight down instead. This is because when in the *rukū*ʿ, the Messenger of Allāh (s) "neither kept his head up nor lowered it" as mentioned in the ḥadīth of ʿĀ'isha (r) cited above.
- For further discussion on this topic, see *Where to Look when in Rukū*ʿ on page 241 in the main book.

Figure 4: The Rukū'

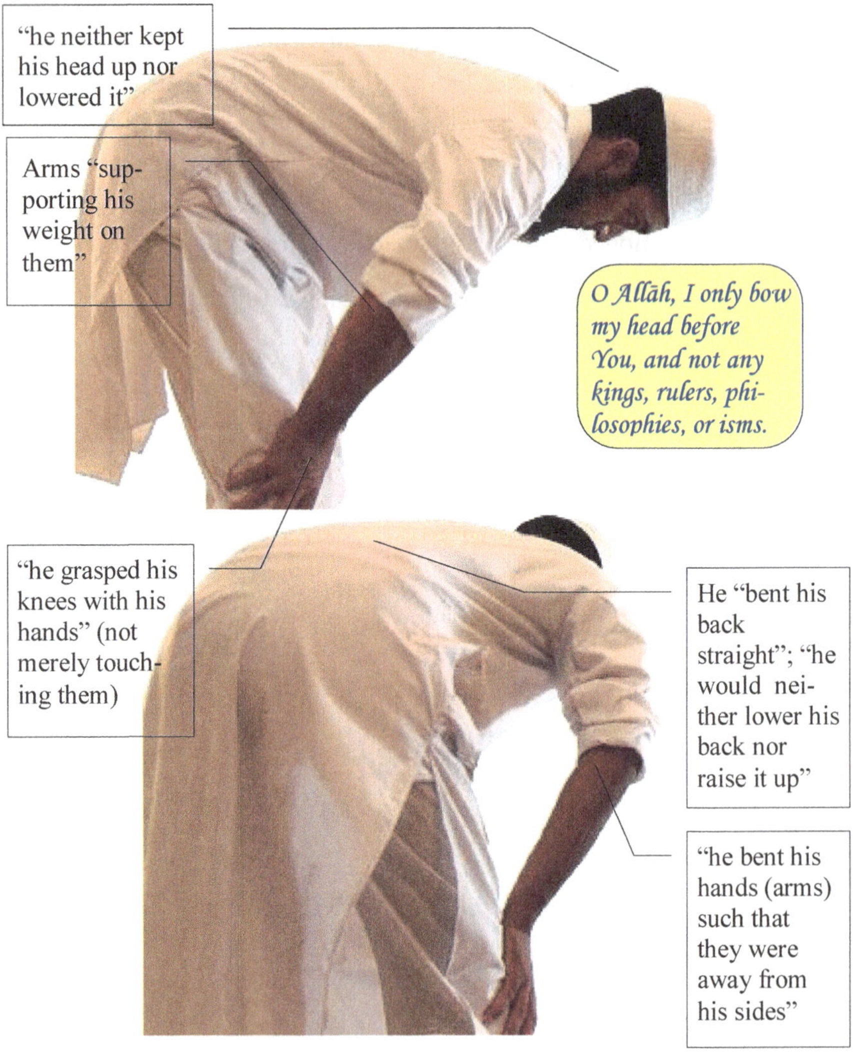

<u>Incorrect practices, or practices that do not have any textual evidence</u>

- Back is arched.
- Head is lower than the back and inclined towards the ground.
- Arms and elbows are close to the sides.

- Hands merely touching the knees, neither grabbing them nor supporting the weight of the back.
- Being quick and always in motion – not allowing several moments to pass in which the body is completely still and relaxed.

Allowing the Body to Come to Full Rest in *Rukū'*, *Sajdah, Qawmah, Jalsah,* etc.

- **Taking time to allow the body to relax**: In each position in the ṣalāh, one should allow the body to stay motionless at least for a few moments so that it is relaxed.
- **Quick movements may invalidate ṣalāh**: The Messenger of Allāh (s) asked a man to repeat his ṣalāh because his movements were apparently too quick. He explained to him how he should make *rukū'*, *sajdah*, standing after *rukū'*, sitting in between the *sujūd*, etc. so that he is completely relaxed.

(This is part of the instructions that the Prophet (s) gave to that man. The ḥadīth is narrated by Rifā'ah bin Rāfi' (r)) "… Then he should say the *takbīr* and make *rukū'* until his joints settle (حتى تطمئن مفاصله) and he is relaxed (وتسترخي). Then he should say *sami' allāhu liman ḥamidah* and stand up straight (يستوي قائما) until he brings his backbone to rest (حتى يقيم صلبه). Then he should say the *takbīr* and make *sajdah* until he has placed his face firmly on the ground (حتى يمكن وجهه) ... (and) his joints settle (حتى تطمئن مفاصله) and he is relaxed (وتسترخي), then he should say the *takbīr* and rise until he comes to rest sitting on his posterior (حتى يستوي قاعدا على مقعدته) and brings his back to rest (ويقيم صلبه). Then he should say the *takbīr* and make *sajdah* until he has placed his face firmly on the ground (حتى يمكن وجهه) and he is relaxed (ويسترخي). If he does not do that then he has not completed his ṣalāh (لم تتم صلاته)." (Nasā'ī, Abū Dāwud)[22]

- **Scholars' opinions**: According to all the *madhhabs* except the Ḥanafī, when returning from the *rukū'* or the *sajdah*, it is obligatory to stand up (or sit up) to an upright position until the body is fully settled and relaxed. The Ḥanafī school considers it obligatory only when sitting up or standing up from the *sajdah.*[23]

- For more ḥadīths and discussion on this, see *Allowing the Body to Come to Full Rest in All Positions* on page 243 in the main book.

Ṣalāh Not Valid If *Rukū'*, *Sajdah*, etc. Are Not Done Properly

- **Quick movements is improper etiquette**: In ṣalāh, one stands in front of Allāh (swt) and offers it for Him only. Therefore, one should maintain proper etiquette and respect in front of the Majesty of Allāh (swt) when he offers his ṣalāh. Making quick movements, as if ṣalāh is a burden and needs to be "gotten over with", is contrary to having such etiquette and respect with Allāh (swt).

- **Quick movements may invalidate ṣalāh**: According to a number of ḥadīths, if one does not take the time to make *rukū'*, *sajdah*, etc. properly, then his ṣalāh may be nullified.

> Anas bin Mālik (r) narrated: The Prophet (s) said, "Perform *rukū'* and *sujūd* properly (أقيموا الركوع و السجود). By Allāh, I can see you behind me – or behind my back – when you make *rukū'* and *sajdah*." (Bukhārī, Muslim)[24]

> Abū Mas'ūd al-Anṣārī (r) narrated: The Messenger of Allāh (s) said, "A person's ṣalāh will not be acceptable in which a man does not bring his backbone to rest (لا يقيم الرجل فيها صلبه) when making *rukū'* and *sujūd*." (Nasā'ī, Abū Dāwud, Ibn Mājah, Tirmidhī)[25]

- For additional ḥadīths and discussion on this, see *Ṣalāh Invalid If Rukū', Sajdah, Standing, etc. Are Not Done Properly* on page 245 in the main book.

Length of Time While in *Rukū'*, *Sajdah, Qawmah,* and *Jalsah*

- **Equal length of time**: According to a number of ḥadīths, the Prophet's (s) time spent in *rukū'*, *qawmah*, *sajdah*, and between the *sujūd* were of almost equal length.

> Al-Barā' bin 'Āzib (r) narrated: "The *rukū'*, the *sujūd*, the period of standing after *rukū'* and the interval between the two *sujūd* of the Prophet (s) used to be almost equal in length (قريبا من السواء)." (Bukhārī, Nasā'ī, Tirmidhī)[26]

- **Longer in nightly voluntary ṣalāh**: Sometimes, during nightly voluntary prayers, he would spend such a long time in *rukū'* that it would be almost as long as his standing.

> Ḥudhaifah (r) narrated: "I prayed with the Prophet (s) one night and he started to recite al-Baqarah ... Then he made *rukū'* ... and his *rukū'* was almost as long as his standing (فكان ركوعه نحوا من قيامه) ... Then he stood for a long time (ثم قام طويلا), almost as long as in *rukū'* (قريبا مما ركع). Then he made *sajdah* ... and his *sujūd* was almost as long as his standing (فكان سجوده نحوا من قيامه) ..." (Muslim, Nasā'ī)[27]

- **Scholars' opinions**: Al-Albānī subscribes to the view that one's *rukū'*, standing after the *rukū'*, *sajdah*, and between the *sujūd* should be all nearly equal in length.[28]

- For additional ḥadīths and discussion about this, see *Length of Time While in Rukū', Qawmah, Sajdah and Jalsah* on page 247 in the main book.

Recitation in the *Rukū'*

- **Option for multiple *adhkār***: There are several *adhkār* from which the Messenger of Allāh (s) used to recite in the *rukū'*. Three of these are mentioned below, where the no. 1 has the most narrations available.

(1)

سُبْحَانَ رَبِّيَ الْعَظِيمِ

Glory to my Lord, the Almighty. (Muslim, Nasā'ī, Tirmidhī)[29]

(2)

سُبْحَانَكَ اَللَّهُمَّ رَبَّنَا وَبِحَمْدِكَ اللَّهُمَّ اغفِرْ لِي

Glory to You O Allāh, Our Lord! And praise is to You.
O Allāh, forgive me! (Bukhārī, Abū Dāwud, Nasā'ī)[30]

(3)

سُبُّوحٌ قُدُّوسٌ رَبُّ المَلائِكَةِ وَ الرُّوحِ

Glorified, Holy, Lord of the Angels and the Spirit.
(Muslim, Abū Dāwud, Nasā'ī)[31]

- For supporting ḥadīths as well as the texts of the other *adhkār*, see *Recitation in the Rukū'* on page 251 in the main book.

When Recitations in *Rukū'* and *Sajdah* Were Initiated

- **Allāh's (swt) commands**: Recitation in *rukū'* and *sajdah* was initiated by the Prophet (s) in response to the following verses:

  فَسَبِّحْ بِاسْمِ رَبِّكَ الْعَظِيمِ

  Then celebrate with praises the Name of thy Lord, the Supreme! (56:74)

  سَبِّحِ اسْمَ رَبِّكَ الْأَعْلَى

  So glorify the Name of thy Lord Most High. (69:52)

- This is based on the following ḥadīth of the Prophet (s):

> 'Uqbah bin 'Āmīr narrated: "When the verse فسبح باسم ربك العظيم (al-Waqi'ah: 74) was revealed, the Messenger of Allāh (s) said, 'Place this in your *rukū'*.' And when the verse سبح اسم ربك الأعلى (al-A'lā: 1) was revealed, he said, 'Place this in your *sajdah*.' " (Abū Dāwud, Ibn Mājah)[32]

- **Response to Allāh's (swt) commands:** So, reciting سبحان ربي العظيم in the *rukū'* corresponds to Allāh's (swt) command فسبح باسم ربك العظيم, and reciting سُبْحَانَ رَبِّيَ الأعْلَى in the *sajdah* corresponds to His (swt) command سبح اسم ربك الأعلى. May He be Glorified and Exalted!

Recitation in *Rukū'* and *Sajdah* to Be Done Three Times

- **Three times**: The ḥadīths about the recitation in *rukū'* and *sajdah* usually focus on what the Prophet (s) recited as opposed to how many times he recited it. There are, however, few narrations available in the *Six Most Authentic Books* regarding the number of times recitation is done in *rukū'* and *sajdah*.

> 'Uqbah bin 'Āmīr (r) narrated: "... when the Messenger of Allāh (s) would go into *rukū'*, he would say three times سبحان ربى العظيم وبحمده, and when he went into *sajdah*, he would say three times سبحان ربي الأعلى وبحمده." (Abū Dāwud)[33]

- **Scholars' opinions**: According to the Ḥanafī, Shāfi'ī, and the Ḥanbalī schools, the Prophetic example is to recite *subḥāna rabbiya-l-'aẓīm* during *rukū'* and *subḥāna rabbiya-l-a'lā* during *sajdah*. Proper emulation of the Sunnah is to recite these at least three times according to the Ḥanafī and Shāfi'ī schools, and "multiple" times according to the Ḥanbalī school.[34]

- For more evidence and discussion on this, see *Recitations in Rukū' and Sajdah to Be Done How Many Times* on page 256 in the main book.

No Qur'ān Recitation in *Rukū'* or *Sajdah*

- **Not permissible**: Reciting Qur'ān during *rukū'* or *sujūd* is not permissible. The Messenger of Allāh (s) said that he was forbidden to recite the Qur'ān when in *rukū'* or *sajdah* and he also forbade the Companions form doing so.

ʿAlī ibn Abī Ṭālib (r) narrated: "The Messenger of Allāh (s) forbade me (نهاني) from reciting the Qur'ān while in *rukūʿ* or *sajdah* (أن أقرأ راكعا أو ساجدا)." (Muslim, Nasā'ī, Tirmidhī)[35]

- For additional ḥadīths on this, see *No Qur'ān Recitation in Rukūʿ or Sajdah* on page 257 in the main book.

---

[1] Bukhārī, *Adhān*, 735-36, 738-39; Muslim, *Ṣalāh*, 861-62; Abū Dāwud, *Ṣalāh*, 721-22, 741-42; Ibn Mājah, *Establishing Ṣalāh*, 858; Nasā'ī, *Commencement of Ṣalāh*, 877-79, 1026; *At-Taṭbīq*, 1058, 1060, 1089, 1145; *Forgetfulness*, 1183; Tirmidhī, *Ṣalāh*, 255-56.

[2] Al-Albānī, *The Prophet's Prayer Described*, p. 42.

[3] Bukhārī, *Adhān*, 735-36, 738-39; Muslim, *Ṣalāh*, 861-62; Abū Dāwud, *Ṣalāh*, 721-22, 741-42; Ibn Mājah, *Establishing Ṣalāh*, 858; Nasā'ī, *Commencement of Ṣalāh*, 877-79, 1026; *At-Taṭbīq*, 1058, 1060, 1089, 1145; *Forgetfulness*, 1183; Tirmidhī, *Ṣalāh*, 255-56.

[4] Muslim, *Ṣalāh*, 896; Abū Dāwud, *Ṣalāh*, 723, 726; Ibn Mājah, *Establishing Ṣalāh*, 867; Nasā'ī, *Commencement of Ṣalāh*, 890; *At-Taṭbīq*, 1056, 1103, 1160; *Forgetfulness*, 1264, 1266.

[5] Ibn Mājah, *Establishing Ṣalāh*, 866.

[6] Abū Dāwud, *Ṣalāh*, 738.

[7] Al-Jazīrī, *Islamic Jurisprudence*, p. 324. According to the Ḥanafī school, hands should be raised only once during the opening *takbīr*. (*Ibid.*, p. 324)

[8] Al-Albānī, *The Prophet's Prayer Described*, p. 42.

[9] Nasā'ī, *At-Taṭbīq*, 1040; Abū Dāwud, *Ṣalāh*, 734; Tirmidhī, *Ṣalāh*, 304-05.

[10] Bukhārī, *Adhān*, 790; Muslim, *Masājid*, 1196; Abū Dāwud, *Ṣalāh*, 867.

[11] Ibn Mājah, *Establishing Ṣalāh*, 1061.

[12] Bukhārī, *Adhān*, 828.

[13] Al-Jazīrī, *Islamic Jurisprudence*, pp. 301, 338, 347.

[14] *Ibid.*, pp. 315, 323.

[15] Abū Dāwud, *Ṣalāh*, 734. Tirmidhī has a *ḥasan* narration about this. See Tirmidhī, *Ṣalāh*, 260.

[16] Al-Jazīrī, *Islamic Jurisprudence*, p. 323.

[17] *Ibid.*, pp. 338, 347.

[18] Nasā'ī, *At-Taṭbīq*, 1040; Ibn Mājah, *Establishing Ṣalāh*, 1061; Abū Dāwud, *Ṣalāh*, 730; Tirmidhī, *Ṣalāh*, 304-05.

---

[19] Bukhārī, *Adhān*, 828.

[20] Muslim, *Ṣalāh,* 1110; Abū Dāwud, *Ṣalāh*, 783; Ibn Mājah, *Establishing Ṣalāh*, 869.

[21] Al-Jazīrī, *Islamic Jurisprudence*, pp. 300-01, 315, 323.

[22] Nasā'ī, *At-Taṭbīq*, 1137; Abū Dāwud, *Ṣalāh*, 857-58; 860. No. 860 is graded *ḥasan*.

[23] Al-Jazīrī, *Islamic Jurisprudence*, pp. 304-05, 309, 311, 315; Muḥammad and Mughniyyah, *Prescribed Prayers*, p. 47.

[24] Bukhārī, *Adhān*, 742; Muslim, *Ṣalāh*, 959.

[25] Nasā'ī, *Commencement of Ṣalāh*, 1028; *At-Taṭbīq*, 1112; Abū Dāwud, *Ṣalāh*, 855; Ibn Mājah, *Establishing Ṣalāh*, 870; Tirmidhī, *Ṣalāh*, 265.

[26] Bukhārī, *Adhān*, 801, 792; Nasā'ī, *At-Taṭbīq*, 1066, 1149; Tirmidhī, *Ṣalāh*, 279-80.

[27] Muslim, *Traveller's Prayer*, 1814; Nasā'ī, *Qiyām al-Lail*, 1665.

[28] Al-Albānī, *The Prophet's Prayer Described*, 46, 50.

[29] Muslim, *Traveller's Prayer*, 1814; Nasā'ī, *Commencement of Ṣalāh*, 1009; *At-Taṭbīq*, 1047, 1070, 1134, 1146; *Qiyām al-Lail*, 1665-66; Tirmidhī, *Ṣalāh*, 262-63.

[30] Bukhārī, *Adhān*, 794, 817; *Commentary*, 4968; Abū Dāwud, *Ṣalāh*, 877; Nasā'ī, *At-Taṭbīq*, 1123-24.

[31] Muslim, *Ṣalāh*, 1091-92; Abū Dāwud, *Ṣalāh*, 872; Nasā'ī, *At-Taṭbīq*, 1049, 1135.

[32] Abū Dāwud, *Ṣalāh*, 869-70; Ibn Mājah, *Establishing Ṣalāh*, 887

[33] Abū Dāwud, *Ṣalāh*, 870.

[34] Al-Jazīrī, *Islamic Jurisprudence*, pp. 313, 315, 321-22, 337.

[35] Muslim, *Ṣalāh*, 1076-79; Nasā'ī, *At-Taṭbīq*, 1119-20; Tirmidhī, *Clothing*, 1737.

Standing up from the *Rukū'* (القومة)

After the *rukū'*, the Messenger of Allāh (s) would stand back up. This brief standing is known as the *qawmah.*

Raising the Hands when Rising from the *Rukū'*

- **Raising the hands**: As he did when he went to the *rukū'*, the Messenger of Allāh (s) would also raise his hands when standing up from the *rukū'*.

- **Many ḥadīths on it**: There are many authentic narrations that prove this practice of the Prophet (s). Some of these have already been cited in *Raising the Hands Before Going to Rukū'* on page 74 above. For more evidence, see *Raising the Hands Before/After Rukū'* on page 209 in the main book.

Allowing the Body to Come to Full Rest While Standing

- **Quick movements may invalidate the ṣalāh**: The Messenger of Allāh (s) asked a man to repeat his ṣalāh because his movements were apparently too quick. He explained to him how he should return from the *rukū'*, saying "then he should say *sami' allāhu liman hamidah* and stand up straight (يستوي قائما) until he brings his backbone to rest (حتى يقيم صلبه)." (Nasā'ī, Abū Dāwud)[1]

- For a fuller text of this ḥadīth, see *Allowing the Body to Come to Full Rest in Rukū', Sajdah, Qawmah, Jalsah, etc.* on page 81 above. For additional ḥadīths and discussion on this topic, see

Allowing the Body to Come to Full Rest in All Positions on page 243 in the main book.

Length of Time While Standing

- **Equal length of time**: It has been reported that the Prophet's (s) *rukūʿ*, *sujūd*, standing after the *rukūʿ* and the time between the two *sujūd* used to be almost equal in length. Sometimes, he would stand for so long that the Companions thought that he had forgotten.

> Al-Barāʾ bin ʿĀzib (r) narrated: "The *rukūʿ*, the *sujūd*, the period of standing after *rukūʿ* and the interval between the two *sujūd* of the Prophet (s) used to be almost equal in length (قريبا من السواء)." (Bukhārī, Nasāʾī, Tirmidhī)[2]

> Anas bin Mālik (r) narrated: "... when the Messenger of Allāh (s) said *samiʿ allāhu liman ḥamidah*, he would stand for so long that we would think he has forgotten (قام، حتى نقول قد أوهم). Then he would make *sajdah*, and he would sit for so long between the *sajdahs* (ويقعد بين السجدتين) that we would think he has forgotten (حتى نقول قد أوهم)." (Muslim, Abū Dāwud)[3]

- For additional ḥadīths and discussion about this, see *Length of Time While in Rukūʿ, Qawmah, Sajdah and Jalsah* on page 247 in the main book.

Recitation in the *Qawmah:* the *Tasmīʿ* and the *Tahmid*

- **The *tasmīʿ* and the *taḥmīd***: Recitation after standing up (*qawmah*) from the *rukūʿ* includes saying the *tasmīʿ* and the *taḥmīd*. The former is the utterance *samiʿ allāhu liman ḥamidah* whereas the latter is *rabbanā (wa) laka-l-ḥamd*, with optionally adding *allāhumma* before it.

- **Depends on whether leading or following**: Whether one says both the *tasmīʿ* and the *taḥmīd* or just one of them depends on whether one is praying alone/leading the ṣalāh as an *imām* or he is following an *imām*.

Recitation when Praying Alone or Leading Others as *Imām*

- **Both to be recited**: When one is praying alone or leading others as *imām*, he should say both the *tasmī*ʿ and the *taḥmīd*.
- **Option for multiple *adhkār***: There are several *adhkār* from which the Messenger of Allāh (s) used to recite in the *qawmah* position. Some of these are mentioned below where the no. 1 and the no. 2 have the most narrations available.

(1)

سَمِعَ اللَّهُ لِمَنْ حَمِدَه، رَبَّنَا وَلَكَ الحَمْدُ

Allāh hears those who praise Him; Our Lord, and to You is the praise. (Bukhārī, Muslim, Nasā'ī, Abū Dāwud, Ibn Mājah)[4]

(2)

سَمِعَ اللَّهُ لِمَنْ حَمِدَه، رَبَّنَا لَكَ الحَمْدُ

Allāh hears those who praise Him; Our Lord, to You is the praise. (Bukhārī, Muslim, Nasā'ī)[5]

(3)

سَمِعَ اللَّهُ لِمَنْ حَمِدَه، اللَّهُمَّ رَبَّنَا وَلَكَ الحَمْدُ

or

سَمِعَ اللَّهُ لِمَنْ حَمِدَه، اللَّهُمَّ رَبَّنَا لَكَ الحَمْدُ

Allāh hears those who praise Him; O Allāh, Our Lord, (and) to You is the praise. (Bukhārī, Nasā'ī, Abū Dāwud)[6]

(4)

rabbanā (wa) laka-l-ḥamd, plus the following addition:

حَمْدًا كَثِيرًا طَيِّبًا مُبَارَكًا فِيهِ

Plentiful, pure, and blessed praise.
(Bukhārī, Nasā'ī, Abū Dāwud)[7]

(5)

رَبَّنَا (وَ) لَكَ الحَمْدُ, plus the following addition:

مِلْءَ السَّمَاوَاتِ وَمِلْءَ الأَرْضِ وَمِلْءَ مَا شِئْتَ مِنْ شَيْءٍ بَعْدُ

Filling the heavens, and filling the earth and filling whatever else You will besides that. (Muslim, Nasā'ī, Abū Dāwud, Ibn Mājah)[8]

- **Scholars' opinions**: According to the Shāfiʿī and Ḥanbalī schools, the Prophetic Sunnah is to say both the *tasmīʿ* and the *taḥmīd* when one is leading as *imām* or praying alone. In the Mālikī school also, it is recommended for the *imām* to say the *taḥmīd* after saying the *tasmīʿ*.[9]
- For supporting ḥadīths as well as the texts of the other *adhkār*, see *Recitation in Qawmah when Praying Alone or Leading Others* on page 267 and *Should the Imām Say samiʿ allāhu liman ḥamidah Only?* on page 283 in the main book.

Recitation in *Qawmah* when Following an *Imām*

- ***Tasmiʿ* not required when following *imām***: When one is following an *imām*, then he is not required to say سمع الله لمن حمده when standing up from *rukūʿ*, as appears to be the case from a number of ḥadīths. Instead, when the *imām* says سمع الله لمن حمده, he may say ربنا لك الحمد or ربنا ولك الحمد, with the option of adding اللهم before it or حمدا كثيرا طيبا مباركا فيه after it.

> Abū Hurairah (r) narrated: The Prophet (s) said, "The *imām* is to be followed. Say the *takbīr* when the *imām* says it, make *rukūʿ* when he makes *rukūʿ*, when he says *samiʿ allāhu liman ḥamidah* (وإذا قال سمع الله لمن حمده), say *rabbanā wa laka-l-ḥamd* (فقولوا ربنا ولك الحمد) ..." (Bukhārī, Ibn Mājah, Tirmidhī)[10]

> ʿĀ'isha (r) narrated: Allāh's Messenger (s) ... said, "The *imām* is to be followed: make *rukūʿ* when he makes *rukūʿ*, raise up your heads when he raises up his head and when he says *samiʿ allāhu liman ḥamidah* (وإذا قال سمع الله لمن حمده), say *rabbanā wa laka-l-ḥamd* (فقولوا ربنا ولك الحمد) ..." (Bukhārī)[11]

- **Scholars' opinions**: The Ḥanafī and the Ḥanbalī schools hold that when the *imām* says *sami῾ allāhu liman ḥamidah*, the followers only say *allāhumma rabbanā wa laka-l-ḥamd*, or *rabbanā wa laka-l-ḥamd*, or *rabbanā laka-l-ḥamd*, the first version being preferable. The Mālikī school also has a similar opinion.[12]
- For further evidence and discussion on this, see *Recitation in Qawmah when Following an Imām* on page 278 in the main book.

---

[1] Nasā'ī, *At-Taṭbīq*, 1137; Abū Dāwud, *Ṣalāh*, 857-58; 860. No. 860 is graded *ḥasan*.

[2] Bukhārī, *Adhān*, 801, 792; Nasā'ī, *At-Taṭbīq*, 1066, 1149; Tirmidhī, *Ṣalāh*, 279-80.

[3] Muslim, *Ṣalāh*, 1061; Abū Dāwud, *Ṣalāh*, 853.

[4] Bukhārī, *Adhān*, 735, 738, 803-04, 789; *Eclipses*, 1046, 1065; Muslim, *Ṣalāh*, 868-70; *Masājid*, 1540-41; *Traveller's Prayer*, 1813; Nasā'ī, *Commencement of Ṣalāh*, 877, 879, 1024; *At-Taṭbīq*, 1075, 1060, 1157; Abū Dāwud, *Ṣalāh*, 836; *Prayer for Rain*, 1180; Ibn Mājah, *Establishing Ṣalāh*, 875, 1263.

[5] Bukhārī, *Adhān*, 789; Muslim, *Traveller's Prayer*, 1814; *Eclipses*, 2091; Nasā'ī, *At-Taṭbīq*, 1058, 1151.

[6] Bukhārī, *Adhān*, 795; Nasā'ī, *At-Taṭbīq*, 1061; Abū Dāwud, *Ṣalāh*, 603-04.

[7] Bukhārī, *Adhān*, 799; Nasā'ī, *At-Taṭbīq*, 1063; Abū Dāwud, *Ṣalāh*, 763, 770.

[8] Muslim, *Ṣalāh*, 1067, 1073; Nasā'ī, *At-Taṭbīq*, 1067; Abū Dāwud, *Ṣalāh*, 846; Ibn Mājah, *Establishing Ṣalāh*, 878.

[9] Al-Jazīrī, *Islamic Jurisprudence*, p. 327.

[10] Bukhārī, *Adhān*, 734; Ibn Mājah, *Establishing Ṣalāh*, 1239; Tirmidhī, *Ṣalāh*, 267.

[11] Bukhārī, *Adhān*, 688.

[12] Al-Jazīrī, *Islamic Jurisprudence*, pp. 326-27. According to the Shāfi῾ī school, both the *imām* and the followers should say the *tasmī῾* and the *taḥmīd*. (*Ibid.*, p. 327.)

The *Sajdah* (السجدة)

After the brief standing in the *qawmah*, the Messenger of Allāh (s) would go to the *sajdah*.

Excellence of Making *Sajdah*

- **List of excellences**: There are many excellences mentioned in the ḥadīth about making *sajdah*. These include:
  - Muslims will be recognized on the Day of Judgment from the "traces of *sujūd*" (ويعرفونهم بآثر السجود) on their heads. (Bukhārī)[1]
  - Hellfire has been forbidden "to consume the traces of *sujūd*" (أن تأكل أثر السجود). (Bukhārī)[2]
  - Every single time a Muslim makes *sajdah*, "Allāh will raise you one degree in status thereby (رفعك الله بها درجة), and erase one sin for you (وحط عنك بها خطيئة)." (Muslim, Nasā'ī, Ibn Mājah, Tirmidhī)[3].
  - Making frequent *sajdah* to Allāh (swt) in ṣalāh facilitates in earning Paradise in the Hereafter and be close to the Prophet (s). (Muslim, Abū Dāwud, Nasā'ī)[4]
  - "The closest that a servant comes to his Lord (أَقْرَبُ مَا يَكُونُ الْعَبْدُ مِنْ رَبِّهِ) is when he is in *sajdah*." (Muslim, Nasā'ī, Abū Dāwud)[5]

- When one supplicates to Allāh (swt) during the *sajdah*, "it is likely that you will be responded to (فَقَمِنٌ أَنْ يُسْتَجَابَ لَكُمْ)." (Muslim, Nasā'ī, Abū Dāwud)[6].

- For the full texts of the ḥadīths that describe the excellence of making *sajdah*, see *Excellence of Making Sajdah* on page 291 and *Making Du'ā' While in Sajdah* on page 317 in the main book.

Saying the *Takbīr* when Going to the First *Sajdah*

- ***Takbīr* when going to the *sajdah***: As one goes to the *sajdah*, he should say the *takbīr*. The Messenger of Allāh (s) instructed the Companions (r): "then say the *takbīr* and make *sajdah*."

> Abū Mūsā al-Ash'arī (r) narrated: "... The Messenger of Allāh (s) addressed us and explained our Sunnah to us and taught us our ṣalāh. He said, "When you offer ṣalāh, make your rows straight and let one of you lead the others ... when he says the *takbīr* and makes *sajdah*, then say the *takbīr* and make *sajdah* (فَكَبِّرُوا وَاسْجُدُوا) ..." (Muslim, Abū Dāwud, Nasā'ī)[7]

- For the full text of this ḥadīth as well as additional ḥadīths on this, see *Ḥadīths on Takbīr when Going to the First Sajdah* on page 206 in the main book.

Going to the *Sajdah* – Placing the Hands First

- **No *ṣaḥīḥ* ḥadīth**: There is no *ṣaḥīḥ* ḥadīth available in the *Six Most Authentic Books* regarding whether one should place the hands first or the knees first on the ground when going to the *sajdah*.

- **Placing the hands first**: However, there is a *ḥasan* ḥadīth available where the Messenger of Allāh (s) disapproved "kneeling like a camel" (meaning, placing the knees first) and another *ḥasan* ḥadīth available where he clearly instructed placing the hands first.

Abū Hurairah (r) narrated: The Messenger of Allāh (s) said, "When one of you makes *sajdah*, let him put his hands down before his knees (فليضع بيده قبل ركبتيه), and not kneel like a camel (ولا يبرك بروك البعير)." (Nasā'ī, Abū Dāwud, both graded *ḥasan*)[8]

- **Scholars' opinions**: According to the Ḥanafī and Mālikī schools, one should place the hands and then the knees when going down to the ground, and do the reverse when getting up. This is also the view of Al-Albānī.[9]
- For more discussion on this, see *Going to the Sajdah – Hands First or Knees First?* on page 294 in the main book.

Figure 5: Going to the Sajdah

Figure 6: Standing up from Sajdah or Sitting

Manner of Making the *Sajdah*

Making *sajdah* properly involves a number of elements that are documented in the ḥadīth. These are described below.

Making *Sajdah* on "Seven Bones"

- **Seven parts to touch the ground**: When one performs the *sajdah*, seven of his body parts should touch the ground, according to a number of ḥadīths. These are: the face (including the forehead and the nose), the two hands, the two knees, and the toes of the two feet.

> ʿAbdullāh ibn ʿAbbās (r) narrated: The Prophet (s) said, "I have been ordered to make *sajdah* on seven bones: on the forehead (عَلَى الْجَبْهَةِ) – and the Prophet pointed towards his nose (وَأَشَارَ بِيَدِهِ عَلَى أَنْفِهِ) – two hands (وَالْيَدَيْنِ), two knees (وَالرُّكْبَتَيْنِ) and the toes of the two feet (وَأَطْرَافِ الْقَدَمَيْنِ), and not to gather the clothes or the hair." (Bukhārī, Muslim, Nasāʾī)[10]

- **Scholars' opinions**: There is some debate among the scholars about whether it is mandatory for the nose to touch the ground, but most scholars, including the Shāfiʿī and the Ḥanbalī schools, agree that the seven body parts mentioned in the ḥadīths above should be on the ground during the *sajdah*.[11]

- For more ḥadīths on this, see *Making Sajdah on "Seven Bones"* on page 296 in the main book.

Forehead and Nose to Touch the Ground

- **Parts of the face that touch the ground**: When making *sajdah*, both the forehead and the nose should touch the ground. This is evident in the ḥadīth cited above. There are also additional narrations that support this.

> [Abū Ḥumaid as-Sāʿidī (r) was demonstrating how the Prophet (s) made ṣalāh] "... Then he made *sajdah* and placed his nose and forehead (on the ground) (فأمكن أنفه وجبهته) ..." (Abū Dāwud)[12]

- **Scholars' opinions**: In the Ḥanafī and the Ḥanbalī schools, both the forehead and the nose should touch the ground. In the Mālikī school, it is obligatory that at least part of the forehead, and recommended that the entire forehead and the nose, touch the ground.[13] In the Shāfi'ī school, it is desirable to allow the nose to the touch the ground.[14] Al-Albānī also has the same view that the nose should touch the ground in addition to the forehead.[15]

- For additional ḥadīths on this, see *Forehead and Nose to Touch the Ground* on page 297 in the main book.

Face Should Be Placed Firmly on the Ground

- **Not a mere touch**: It is not sufficient for the face to just lightly touch the ground. It should be firmly placed on the ground, which is necessary for the body to have full balance and be in a relaxed state.

> Rifā'ah bin Rāfi' (r) narrated: [The Prophet (s) was instructing a man how to make ṣalāh properly] "…Then he should say the *takbīr* and make *sajdah* until he has placed his face firmly on the ground (حتى يمكن وجهه) ..." (Nasā'ī, Abū Dāwud)[16]

- **Scholars' opinions**: According to the Mālikī school, it is recommended to place the forehead firmly on the ground.[17]

- For the full text of this ḥadīth, see *Face Should Be Placed Firmly on the Ground* on page 299 in the main book.

Hands to Be Placed on the Ground

- **Hands on the ground**: The hands are part of the "seven bones" that need to be on the ground when one makes *sajdah*.

> 'Abdullāh ibn 'Umar (r) narrated: "The hands make *sajdah* (إِنَّ الْيَدَيْنِ تَسْجُدَانِ) as the face makes *sajdah*; so when one of you puts his face down, he should put his hands down (فَلْيَضَعْ يَدَيْهِ), and when he raises (the face), he should raise (the hands) too." (*marfū'* ḥadīth) (Nasā'ī)[18]

- For additional ḥadīths on this, see *Hands to Be Placed on the Ground* on page 299 in the main book.

Position of the Hands on the Ground

- **On both sides of the face**: According to most of the available narrations, the hands (i.e., the palms) should be placed on both sides of the head/face during the *sajdah*.

> Wā'il bin Ḥujr (r) narrated: "… When he [the Prophet (s)] went to *sajdah*, he made *sajdah* between his hands (سَجَدَ بَيَنَ كَفَّيهِ)." (Muslim)[19]

- **At the level of the shoulders**: There is also a ḥadīth that mentions that the hands should be placed at the level of the shoulders.

> Abū Ḥumaid as-Sāʿidī (r) narrated: "... Then he (s) made *sajdah*, and placed his nose and forehead (on the ground) and kept his hands (arms) at a distance from his sides, and he placed his palms at the level of his shoulders (وَضَعَ كَفَّيْهِ حَذْوَ مَنْكِبَيْهِ) ..." (Abū Dāwud)[20]

- **Reconciled view**: Both of these positions can be reconciled when one performs *sajdah* and places the hands in such a way that the lower part of his palms and wrists are parallel to the shoulders and the upper part of the palms (i.e., the fingers) are parallel to the ears.

- **Scholars' opinions**: Sayyid Sabiq's (r) opinion is that one may place the hands either parallel to the ears or the shoulders, but goes on to say that "Some scholars combine these two acts by placing the ends of the thumbs parallel to the ears and the palms parallel to the shoulders."[21] According to the Mālikī school, one should place the hands alongside the ears. In the Ḥanafī school, the Prophetic example is to place the hands parallel to either the head or the shoulders.[22]

- For additional ḥadīths and discussion on this subject, see *Where to Place the Hands on the Ground* on page 300 in the main book.

Fingers to Be Straight Towards the *Qiblah*

- **Fingers point to the *qiblah***: When making *sajdah*, one should place the hands on the grounds in a way so that the fingers remain straight towards the *qiblah*.

> Abū Ḥumaid as-Sāʿidī (r) narrated: When he (s) made *sajdah*, he placed both his hands (on the ground) without sticking them out or tucking them close, and he made his fingers point towards the *qiblah* (وَاسْتَقْبَلَ بِأَطْرَافِ أَصَابِعِهِ الْقِبْلَةَ). (Abū Dāwud)[23]

- **In a natural state**: The above ḥadīth also indicates that one should not spread the fingers too wide, for that would make all the fingers, except the middle finger, stray from the direction of the *qiblah*. Instead, one should keep the fingers in a natural state – neither sticking them together by force, nor spreading them wide.

- **Scholars' opinions**: According to the Mālikī, Shāfiʿī, and the Ḥanbalī schools, the fingers should be closed and point towards the *qiblah*.[24]

Elbows to Not Touch the Ground

- **Above the ground**: The Prophet (s) explicitly prohibited placing the arms and the elbows on the ground when making *sajdah*.

> Anas bin Mālik (r) narrated: The Prophet (s) said, "Be balanced in *sujūd* and let not any of you spread his forearms (along the ground) like a dog (وَلَا يَبْسُطْ أَحَدُكُمْ ذِرَاعَيْهِ انْبِسَاطَ الْكَلْبِ)." (Bukhārī, Muslim, Nasā'ī, Abū Dāwud, Ibn Mājah, Tirmidhī)[25]

> Al-Barā' bin ʿĀzib (r) narrated: The Messenger of Allāh (s) said, "When you make *sajdah*, place your palms (on the ground) and raise your elbows (فَضَعْ كَفَّيْكَ وَارْفَعْ مِرْفَقَيْكَ)." (Muslim)[26]

- **Scholars' opinions**: In the Ḥanafī and the Ḥanbalī schools, the Sunnah is to keep the arms off the ground during the *sajdah.*[27]
- For more evidence and discussion on this, see *Elbows to Not Touch the Ground* on page 303 in the main book.

Arms to Be Away from the Sides

- **Widening the arms**: During the *sajdah*, one should hold his arms away from his sides to the extent that his armpits would become visible from behind if he is not wearing a sleeved garment.

> ʿAbdullāh bin Mālik (r) narrated: "Whenever the Prophet (s) offered ṣalāh, he (during *sajdah*) used to separate his arms from his body so widely that (فَرَّجَ بَيْنَ يَدَيْهِ حَتَّى) the whiteness of his armpits would be visible (يَبْدُوَ بَيَاضُ إِبْطَيْهِ)." (Bukhārī, Muslim, Nasā'ī)[28]

> Maimunah bint al-Ḥārith (r) narrated: "When the Messenger of Allāh (s) made *sajdah*, he kept his arms so far apart that (خَوَّى بِيَدَيْهِ تَعْنِي جَنَّحَ حَتَّى) the whiteness of his armpits could be seen from behind (يُرَى وَضَحُ إِبْطَيْهِ مِنْ وَرَائِهِ)." (Muslim, Nasā'ī)[29]

- **Being considerate to others**: This should, however, be practiced when there is sufficient room available on both sides, such as when one is praying alone or leading as *imām*.
- **Scholars' opinions**: The Ḥanafī, Mālikī, and the Ḥanbalī schools agree that the elbows should be away from the sides when making *sajdah.*[30] According to Imām Tirmidhī, keeping the arms away from the sides during the *sajdah* is "acted by the people of knowledge."[31]
- For additional ḥadīths and discussion on this, see *Arms to Be Away from the Sides* on page 304 in the main book.

Thighs to Not Touch Each Other and Be Away from the Belly

- **Gap between thighs/belly**: When in *sajdah*, the thighs should have a gap in between and they should be away from the belly.

> Abū Ḥumaid as-Sāʿidī (r) narrated: "... and when he (s) made *sajdah*, he made a gap between his two thighs (فَرَّجَ بَيْنَ فَخِذَيْهِ), without allowing his stomach to touch the thighs (غَيْرَ حَامِلٍ بَطْنَهُ عَلَى شَيْءٍ مِنْ فَخِذَيْهِ)." (Abū Dāwud)[32]

- **Scholars' opinions**: According to the Ḥanbalī school, the Prophetic example is to keep the knees apart and the thighs away from the abdomen during the *sajdah*.[33] The Mālikī school views this as recommended.[34] In the Ḥanafī school, it is Sunnah for men to keep the thighs away from the belly.[35]
- For additional ḥadīths, see *Thighs to Be Away from the Belly* and *Leaving a Gap Between the Thighs* on pg. 308 in the main book.

Feet Vertical and Toes to Face the *Qiblah*

- **Toes face the *qiblah***: When the Prophet (s) made *sajdah*, he held his feet upright and bent his toes towards the *qiblah*.

> Abū Ḥumaid as-Sāʿidī (r) narrated: "... When he (the Prophet) made *sajdah*, he (s) placed both his hands on the ground with the forearms away from the ground and away from his body, and the tips of his toes were facing the *qiblah* (وَاسْتَقْبَلَ بِأَطْرَافِ أَصَابِعِ رِجْلَيْهِ الْقِبْلَةَ) ..." (Bukhārī)[36]

> ʿĀ'isha (r) narrated: "I missed the Messenger of Allāh (s) one night, so I searched in the *masjid*, and found him in *sajdah* – his feet were held upright (وَقَدَمَاهُ مَنْصُوبَتَانِ) ..." (Abū Dāwud, Nasā'ī)[37]

- **Scholars' opinions**: According to the Ḥanbalī school, the Sunnah, when making the *sajdah*, is to keep the feet vertical and the balls of the feet on the ground, and spread the toes.[38] This would, obviously, make the toes bent towards the *qiblah*.
- For additional ḥadīths on this, see *Feet Upright and Toes to Face the Qiblah* on page 308 in the main book.

Figure 7: The Sajdah

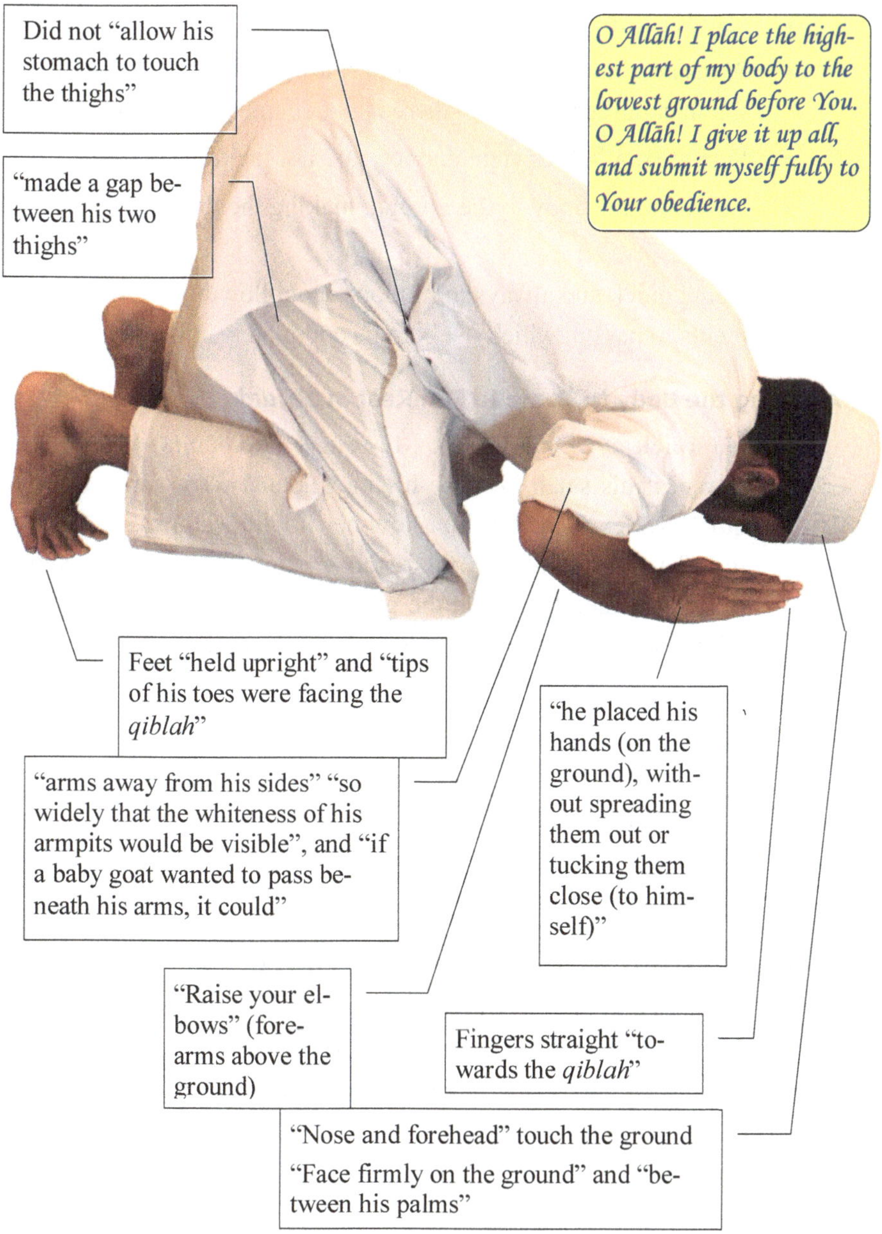

Incorrect practices, or practices that do not have any textual evidence

- Nose does not touch the ground.
- Hands are too close to the face or too far out.
- Arms are close to or touching the sides (acceptable during praying in congregation when there is not enough space in between).
- Feet are not held upright and toes are not facing the *qiblah*.
- Lowering the body to the ground, making the thighs touch the belly.
- Being quick and always in motion – not allowing several moments to pass in which the body is completely still and relaxed.

Allowing the Body to Come to Full Rest in *Sajdah*

- **No quick movements**: The Messenger of Allāh (s) asked a man to repeat his ṣalāh because his movements were apparently too quick. He explained to him how he should perform *sajdah*, saying "Then he should say the *takbīr* and make *sajdah* until he has placed his face firmly on the ground (حتى يمكن وجهه) ... (and) his joints settle (حتى تطمئن مفاصله) and he is relaxed (وتسترخي)." (Nasā'ī, Abū Dāwud)[39]

- For a fuller text of this ḥadīth, see *Allowing the Body to Come to Full Rest in Rukū', Sajdah, Qawmah, Jalsah, etc.* on page 81 above. For additional ḥadīths and discussion on this topic, see *Allowing the Body to Come to Full Rest in All Positions* on page 243 in the main book.

Ṣalāh Not Valid If *Sajdah* Is Not Done Properly

If one does not take the time to make *rukū'* and *sajdah* properly, then his ṣalāh may be nullified. See *Ṣalāh Not Valid If Rukū', Sajdah, etc. Are Not Done Properly* on page 81 above for a supporting ḥadīth on this.

Length of Time While in *Sajdah*

- **Equal length of time**: It has been reported that the Prophet's (s) *rukū'*, *sujūd*, standing after the *rukū'* and the time between the two *sujūd* were of similar length.

- For supporting ḥadīths on this, see *Length of Time While in Rukū', Sajdah, Qawmah, and Jalsah* on page 83 above.

Recitation in the *Sajdah*

- **Response to Allāh's (swt) commands**: The Messenger of Allāh (s) initiated recitation in *rukū'* and *sajdah* in response to the verses فسبح باسم ربك العظيم (al-Waqi'ah: 74) and سبح اسم ربك الأعلى (al-A'lā: 1), as has already been discussed in *When Recitations in Rukū' and Sajdah Were Initiated* on page 84 above.

- **Option for multiple *adhkār***: There are several *adhkār* from which the Messenger of Allāh (s) used to recite in the *sajdah*. Three of these are mentioned below, where the no. 1 has the most narrations available.

(1)

سُبْحَانَ رَبِّيَ الأعْلَى

Glory be to my Lord, the Most High.
(Muslim, Nasā'ī, Abū Dāwud, Tirmidhī)[40]

(2)

سُبْحَانَكَ اَللَّهُمَّ رَبَّنَا وَبِحَمْدِكَ اللَّهُمَّ اغفِرْ لِي

Glory to You O Allāh, Our Lord! And praise is to You. O Allāh, forgive me! (Bukhārī, Abū Dāwud, Nasā'ī)[41]

(3)

سُبُّوحٌ قُدُّوسٌ رَبُّ الْمَلَاءِكَتِ وَ الرُّوحِ

Glorified, Holy, Lord of the Angels and the Spirit.
(Muslim, Abū Dāwud, Nasā'ī)[42]

- For supporting ḥadīths as well as the texts of the other *adhkār*, see *Recitation in Sajdah* on page 311 in the main book.

Recitation in *Sajdah* to Be Done Three Times

See *Recitation in Rukūʿ and Sajdah to Be Done Three Times* on page 85 above for discussion on this.

Making *Duʿā'* While in *Sajdah*

- **Personal *duʿā'* in *sajdah***: One may make personal supplications to Allāh (swt) or praise and glorify Him using his own words. In fact, one is closest to Allāh (swt) and most intimate with Him during the *sajdah*, and hence this is one of the best times to make supplications.

> Abū Hurairah (r) narrated: The Messenger of Allāh (s) said, "The closest that a servant comes to his Lord (أَقْرَبُ مَا يَكُونُ الْعَبْدُ مِنْ رَبِّهِ) is when he is in *sajdah*. Therefore, increase your supplication (at this time) (فَأَكْثِرُوا الدُّعَاءَ)." (Muslim, Nasā'ī, Abū Dāwud)[43]

- ***Duʿā'* in non-Arabic language**: Scholars differ on whether one can make personal *duʿā'* in *sajdah* in his native non-Arabic tongue. The most sound opinion is that it is allowed since there is no textual evidence available that prohibits one from doing so.
- **Scholars' opinions**: According to the Shāfiʿī school, it is Sunnah to make *duʿā'* while in *sajdah*.[44]
- For additional ḥadīths on this, see *Making Duʿā' While in Sajdah* on page 317 in the main book. See also *Can One Make Duʿā' in His Native Tongue While in Sajdah?* on page 318 in the main book.

No Qur'ān Recitation in *Sajdah*

It is not permissible to recite Qur'ān during the *rukūʿ* or the *sajdah*. See *No Qur'ān Recitation in Rukūʿ or Sajdah* on page 85 above for evidence on this.

[1] Bukhārī, *Adhān*, 806.

[2] Bukhārī, *Adhān*, 806.

[3] Muslim, *Ṣalāh*, 1093; Ibn Mājah, *Establishing Ṣalāh*, 1422-23; Nasā'ī, *At-Taṭbīq*, 1140; Tirmidhī, *Ṣalāh*, 388.

[4] Muslim, *Ṣalāh*, 1094; Abū Dāwud, *Voluntary Prayers*, 1320; Nasā'ī, *At-Taṭbīq*, 1139.

[5] Muslim, *Ṣalāh*, 1083; Nasā'ī, *At-Taṭbīq*, 1138; Abū Dāwud, *Ṣalāh*, 875.

[6] Muslim, *Ṣalāh*, 1074-75; Nasā'ī, *At-Taṭbīq*, 1046, 1121; Abū Dāwud, *Ṣalāh*, 876.

[7] Muslim, *Ṣalāh*, 904; Abū Dāwud, *Ṣalāh*, 972-73; Nasā'ī, *Leading Ṣalāh*, 831; *At-Taṭbīq*, 1065, 1173; *Forgetfulness*, 1281.

[8] Nasā'ī, *At-Taṭbīq*, 1092; Abū Dāwud, *Ṣalāh*, 840; both are graded *ḥasan*.

[9] Al-Jazīrī, *Islamic Jurisprudence*, pp. 316, 338, 347; Al-Albānī, *The Prophet's Prayer Described*, p. 52. According to the Shāfi'ī and Ḥanbalī schools, one should place the knees first and then the hands when going down on the ground. (See Al-Misrī, *Reliance of the Traveller*, p. 138; Al-Jazīrī, *Islamic Jurisprudence*, p. 323.)

[10] Bukhārī, *Adhān*, 812; Muslim, *Ṣalāh*, 1098-99; Nasā'ī, *At-Taṭbīq*, 1097-98.

[11] Al-Jazīrī, *Islamic Jurisprudence*, pp. 302, 323.

[12] Abū Dāwud, *Ṣalāh*, 734.

[13] Al-Jazīrī, *Islamic Jurisprudence*, pp. 301-02, 312, 323.

[14] Al-Misrī, *Reliance of the Traveller*, p. 138.

[15] Al-Albānī, *The Prophet's Prayer Described*, p. 53.

[16] Nasā'ī, *At-Taṭbīq*, 1137; Abū Dāwud, *Ṣalāh*, 858.

[17] Al-Jazīrī, *Islamic Jurisprudence*, p. 347.

[18] Nasā'ī, *At-Taṭbīq*, 1093. *Marfū'* is a category of ḥadīth in which the statement or the action is attributed to Prophet Muḥammad (s).

[19] Muslim, *Ṣalāh*, 896.

[20] Abū Dāwud, *Ṣalāh*, 734.

[21] Sabiq, *Fiqh us-Sunnah*, vol. 1, p. 152.

[22] Al-Jazīrī, *Islamic Jurisprudence*, pp. 316, 338, 347. According to the Shāfi'ī and Ḥanbalī schools, the hands should be placed alongside the shoulders. (*Ibid.*, p. 323.)

[23] Abū Dāwud, *Ṣalāh*, 732.

[24] Al-Jazīrī, *Islamic Jurisprudence*, pp. 338-39.

[25] Bukhārī, *Adhān*; 822; *Times of Ṣalāh*, 532; Muslim, *Ṣalāh*, 1102-03; Nasā'ī, *Commencement of Ṣalāh*, 1029; *At-Taṭbīq*, 1111; Ibn Mājah, *Establishing Ṣalāh*, 892; Tirmidhī, *Ṣalāh*, 276.

[26] Muslim, *Ṣalāh*, 1104.

[27] Al-Jazīrī, *Islamic Jurisprudence*, p. 323.

[28] Bukhārī, *Ṣalāh*, 390; Muslim, *Ṣalāh*, 1105-06; Nasā'ī, *At-Taṭbīq*, 1107.

[29] Muslim, *Ṣalāh*, 1108-09; Nasā'ī, *At-Taṭbīq*, 1148.

[30] Al-Jazīrī, *Islamic Jurisprudence*, pp. 316, 323, 348.

[31] Tirmidhī, *Ṣalāh*, 274.

[32] Abū Dāwud, *Ṣalāh*, 735.

[33] Al-Jazīrī, *Islamic Jurisprudence*, p. 323.

[34] *Ibid.*, p. 348.

[35] *Ibid.*, p. 316.

[36] Bukhārī, *Adhān*, 828.

[37] Abū Dāwud, *Ṣalāh*, 879; Nasā'ī, *At-Taṭbīq*, 1101.

[38] Al-Jazīrī, *Islamic Jurisprudence*, p. 323.

[39] Nasā'ī, *At-Taṭbīq*, 1137; Abū Dāwud, *Ṣalāh*, 857-58; 860. No. 860 is graded *ḥasan*.

[40] Muslim, *Traveller's Prayer*, 1814; Nasā'ī, *Commencement of Ṣalāh*, 1009; *At-Taṭbīq*, 1047, 1070, 1134, 1146; *Qiyām al-Lail*, 1665-66; Abū Dāwud, *Ṣalāh*, 871, 874; Tirmidhī, *Ṣalāh*, 262-63.

[41] Bukhārī, *Adhān*, 794, 817; *Commentary*, 4968; Abū Dāwud, *Ṣalāh*, 877; Nasā'ī, *At-Taṭbīq*, 1123-24.

[42] Muslim, *Ṣalāh*, 1091-92; Abū Dāwud, *Ṣalāh*, 872; Nasā'ī, *At-Taṭbīq*, 1049, 1135.

[43] Muslim, *Ṣalāh*, 1083; Nasā'ī, *At-Taṭbīq*, 1138; Abū Dāwud, *Ṣalāh*, 875.

[44] Al-Jazīrī, *Islamic Jurisprudence*, p. 322.

The Sitting in Between the Two *Sajdahs* (الجلسة بين السجدتين)

The Prophet (s) would say the *takbīr* when he rose from the first *sajdah*. He would then sit briefly, say the *takbīr*, and go to the second *sajdah*. This brief sitting between the two *sajdahs* is known as the *jalsah*.

Takbīr when Sitting up from the First *Sajdah*

- ***Takbīr* when rising**: When one raises his head from the first *sajdah*, he should say the *takbīr*.

> Abū Hurairah (r) described the ṣalāh of the Messenger of Allāh (s): "... Then he would say the *takbīr* when going down on the ground (for the first *sajdah*), then he would say the *takbīr* when raising his head (from *sajdah*) (ثُمَّ يُكَبِّرُ حِينَ يَرْفَعُ رَأْسَهُ) ..." (Bukhārī, Nasā'ī)[1]

- For the full text of this ḥadīth as well as additional ḥadīths on this, see *Ḥadīths on Takbīr when Sitting up from the First Sajdah* on page 207 in the main book.

Manner of Sitting Between the *Sujūd*

- ***Iftirāsh* sitting**: Sitting in between the *sujūd* is similar to the general sitting in ṣalāh, called the *iftirāsh* sitting, which is to sit on the left leg with the right foot held vertical.

> Abū Ḥumaid as-Sā'idī narrated that after the first *sajdah*, the Prophet (s) "would raise his head and place his left foot horizontally (on the ground) and sit on it (وَيَثْنِي رِجْلَهُ الْيُسْرَى فَيَقْعُدُ عَلَيْهَا) ... then he would make *sajdah* (again) ..." (Ibn Mājah, Abū Dāwud, Tirmidhī)[2]

- ***Iq'ā'* sitting**: Alternatively, one may also sit in the *iq'ā'* position (sitting on the heels) between the *sujūd*.

> Ṭāwus said: We asked Ibn ʿAbbās about sitting on the heels (الإقْعاءِ عَلَى القَدَمَيْنِ) during (between) *sujūd*, and he said, "It is the Sunnah." So we said, "We see this (position) to be unrefined for a man." Ibn ʿAbbās replied, "This is the Sunnah of your Prophet (s)." (Abū Dāwud, Muslim, Tirmidhī)[3]

- **Scholars' opinions**: According to Al-Albānī and the Shāfiʿī school, one may sit in both *iftirāsh* and *iq'ā'* position between the *sujūd*.[4] Sayyid Sabiq also has the same view.[5]
- For additional ḥadīths and discussion on this, see *Manner of Sitting Between the Sujūd* on page 324 in the main book.

Body Must Come to Full Rest During Sitting Between *Sujūd*

- **Body to be relaxed**: It is important to spend a few moments and allow the body to come to full rest while sitting in between the *sujūd*. The Messenger of Allāh (s) asked a man to repeat his ṣalāh because his movements were apparently too quick. He explained to him how he should make the ṣalāh movements and said, "then he should say the *takbīr* and rise (after the first *sajdah*) until he comes to rest sitting on his posterior (حتى يستوي قاعدا على مقعدته) and brings his back to rest (ويقيم صلبه). Then he should say the *takbīr* and make *sajdah* (again)." (Nasā'ī, Abū Dāwud)[6]
- For a fuller text of this ḥadīth, see *Allowing the Body to Come to Full Rest While Standing* on page 81 above. For additional ḥadīths and discussion on this topic, see *Allowing the Body to Come to Full Rest in All Positions* on page 243 in the main book.

Length of Time While Sitting in Between the *Sujūd*

It has been reported that the Prophet's (s) *rukūʿ*, *sujūd*, standing after the *rukūʿ* and the time between the two *sujūd* would be of similar length. For supporting ḥadīths on this, see *Length of Time While in Rukūʿ, Sajdah, Qawmah, and Jalsah* on page 83 above.

Recitation While Sitting in Between the *Sujūd*

- **Option for multiple *adhkār***: The following are among the *adhkār* that the Messenger of Allāh (s) used to recite in between the *sujūd*, the no. 1 being the most authentic:

(1)

رَبِّ اغْفِرْ لِي، رَبِّ اغْفِرْ لِي

Lord, forgive me! Lord, forgive me!
(Nasā'ī, Abū Dāwud, Ibn Mājah)[7]

(2)

اللَّهُمَّ اغْفِرْ لِي وَارْحَمْنِي وَعَافِنِي وَاهْدِنِي وَارْزُقْنِي

O Allāh! Forgive me, and have mercy on me, and grant me well-being, and guide me, and give me sustenance.
(Abū Dāwud, graded *ḥasan*)[8]

- **Scholars' opinions**: According to the Ḥanbalī school, the Prophetic example is to say *rabbighfirlī* multiple times during the sitting between the *sujūd*.[9]

- For the full texts of the ḥadīths, see *Recitation While Sitting Between the Sujūd* on page 326 in the main book.

Saying the *Takbīr* when Going to the Second *Sajdah*

- ***Takbīr* for the second *sajdah***: The Messenger of Allāh (s) would then say the *takbīr* and go to the second *sajdah*.

> Abū Ḥumaid as-Sāʿidī (r) observed the ṣalāh of the Messenger of Allāh (s): " ... He would then go down on the ground (for the first *sajdah*) ... Then he would raise his head ... Then he would make *sajdah* (again) and say *allāhu akbar* (ثُمَّ يَسْجُدُ ثُمَّ يَقُولُ : اللهُ أَكْبَرُ) ..." (Abū Dāwud, Ibn Mājah)[10]

- For the full text of this ḥadīth as well as additional ḥadīths on this, see *Ḥadīths on Takbīr when Going to the Second Sajdah* on page 207 in the main book.

Saying the *Takbīr* when Rising from the Second *Sajdah*

- ***Takbīr* when rising**: As he rose from the second *sajdah*, the Messenger of Allāh (s) would say the *takbīr* again.

> Abū Hurairah (r) observed the ṣalāh of the Messenger of Allāh (s): "... then he would say the *takbīr* when making *sajdah* (again), then he would say the *takbīr* when raising his head (from the second *sajdah*) (ثُمَّ يُكَبِّرُ حِينَ يَرْفَعُ رَأْسَهُ) ..." (Bukhārī, Nasā'ī)[11]

- For the full text of this ḥadīth as well as additional ḥadīths on this, see *Ḥadīths on Takbīr when Rising from the Second Sajdah* on page 208 in the main book.

Briefly Sitting During the Odd *Rak'ahs* (جلسة الإستراحة)

- **Sitting momentarily**: After the second *sajdah*, the Messenger of Allāh (s) would sometimes sit momentarily before getting up during the odd *rak'ahs* (i.e., the first and the third *rak'ah*). This brief sitting is called *Jalsatu-l-Istirāḥah*, or the sitting of rest.

> Mālik bin Ḥuwairith (r) narrated: "I saw the Prophet (s) offering ṣalāh, and he would not stand up (لَمْ يَنْهَضْ) from any odd (*rak'ah*) of his ṣalāh (فِي وِتْرٍ مِنْ صَلَاتِهِ) that he was in until he had sat down completely (حَتَّى يَسْتَوِيَ قَاعِدًا)." (Bukhārī, Abū Dāwud, Nasā'ī, Tirmidhī)[12]

- **Not always practiced**: This was perhaps not a regular practice of the Messenger of Allāh (s). Most of the ḥadīths that describe the Prophet's (s) ṣalāh do not mention this brief sitting. Additionally, there is a ḥadīth available with contrary evidence, showing that the Messenger of Allāh (s) stood up without this brief sitting.

Abū Ḥumaid as-Sāʿidī (r) narrated: "... and he (the Prophet) made *sajdah*. He positioned himself on his palms, knees, and the toes of his feet. Then he sat sitting on his buttocks (*at-tawarruk*), planting the other foot (right foot) straight. Then he said the *takbīr* and made *sajdah* (again), then he said the *takbīr* and stood up (ثُمَّ كَبَّرَ فقامَ), without sitting on his buttocks (ولَمْ يَتَوَرَّكْ) ..." (Abū Dāwud)[13]

- **Scholars' opinions**: According to the majority of the scholars, including Imām Abū Ḥanīfah, Imām Mālik, some reports from Imam Aḥmad, and others, sitting briefly in the odd rakʿahs is not an "emphasized Sunnah." Rather, it was done out of need since Mālik bin Ḥuwairith (r) observed this practice towards the end of the Prophet (s) life "when his body became heavy."[14] According to the Shāfiʿī school, it is Sunnah to perform this sitting between the first and the second *rakʿah* and the third and the fourth *rakʿah*.[15]

- For more ḥadīths and detailed discussion on this subject, see *Briefly Sitting During the Odd Rakʿahs* on page 327 in the main book.

Standing up After *Sujūd* or Sitting – Lifting the Knees First

- **Lifting the knees first**: When standing up after the second *sajdah* or the first sitting, the closest practice to the Prophetic example is to lift the knees first and then the hands.

- See *Going to the Sajdah – Placing the Hands First* on page 94 above for evidence on this.

- See *Figure 6* on page 96 for illustration.

[1] Bukhārī, *Adhān*, 789; Nasā'ī, *At-Taṭbīq*, 1151.

[2] Ibn Mājah, *Establishing Ṣalāh*, 1061; Abū Dāwud, *Ṣalāh*, 963-65, 967; Tirmidhī, *Ṣalāh*, 304-05.

[3] Abū Dāwud, *Ṣalāh*, 845; Muslim, *Masājid*, 1198; Tirmidhī, *Ṣalāh*, 283.

[4] Al-Albānī, *The Prophet's Prayer Described*, pp. 60-61; Al-Misrī, *Reliance of the Traveller*, pp. 139-40.

[5] Sabiq, *Fiqh us-Sunnah*, vol. 1, p. 155. Sabiq, unfortunately, used an incorrect term – *if'a* – to refer to *iq'ā'* while using *iq'ā'* to refer to another position disliked by the Prophet (s).

[6] Nasā'ī, *At-Taṭbīq*, 1137; Abū Dāwud, *Ṣalāh*, 857-58; 860. No. 860 is graded *ḥasan*.

[7] Nasā'ī, *At-Taṭbīq*, 1070, 1146; *Qiyām al-Lail*, 1666; Abū Dāwud, *Ṣalāh*, 874; Ibn Mājah, *Establishing Ṣalāh*, 897.

[8] Abū Dāwud, *Ṣalāh*, 850, graded *ḥasan*.

[9] Al-Jazīrī, *Islamic Jurisprudence*, pp. 313, 322.

[10] Abū Dāwud, *Ṣalāh*, 730; Ibn Mājah, *Establishing Ṣalāh*, 862, 1061.

[11] Bukhārī, *Adhān*, 789; Nasā'ī, *At-Taṭbīq*, 1151.

[12] Bukhārī, *Adhān*, 823; Abū Dāwud, *Ṣalāh*, 844; Nasā'ī, *At-Taṭbīq*, 1153; Tirmidhī, *Ṣalāh*, 287.

[13] Abū Dāwud, *Ṣalāh*, 966.

[14] Al-Musnad, Muhammad bin 'Abdul-'Aziz (Ed.), *Fatāwā Islāmiyah: Islamic Verdicts From the Noble Scholars 'Abdullah bin Bāz, Ṣaliḥ al-'Uthaymīn, 'Abdur-Raḥmān al-Jibreen*, vol. 2, pp. 166-67.

[15] Al-Jazīrī, *Islamic Jurisprudence*, p. 318.

The First Sitting (الجلوس الأول)

If the ṣalāh has three or four *rak'ahs* in it, then the Messenger of Allāh (s) would sit after the second *rak'ah*.

Manner of the First Sitting (افتراش)

- ***Iftirāsh* sitting**: During the first sitting, the Messenger of Allāh (s) would sit in a manner that is called the *iftirāsh* sitting. There are many ḥadīths that describe this sitting. These ḥadīths contain texts that either directly mention or indicate the following aspects of the *iftirāsh* sitting:
  - **Left foot laid on the ground**: The Messenger of Allāh (s) "would place his left foot horizontally (along the ground) (يَفْرِشُ رِجْلَهُ الْيُسْرَى)" (Muslim, Abū Dāwud)[1] and "sit on his left foot (جَلَسَ عَلَى رِجْلِهِ الْيُسْرَى)." (Bukhārī, Abū Dāwud)[2]
  - **Right foot held upright, toes face the *qiblah***: He would "hold his right foot upright (وَيَنْصِبُ رِجْلَهُ الْيُمْنَى)" (Muslim, Bukhārī, Abū Dāwud)[3] and make "the toes of the right foot face the *qiblah* (وَأَقْبَلَ بِصَدْرِ الْيُمْنَى عَلَى قِبْلَتِهِ)." (Abū Dāwud)[4]
  - **Palms near the knees**: He (s) "would place his right hand on his right thigh (وَضَعَ كَفَّهُ الْيُمْنَى عَلَى فَخِذِهِ الْيُمْنَى)" and "his left hand on his left thigh (وَوَضَعَ كَفَّهُ الْيُسْرَى عَلَى فَخِذِهِ الْيُسْرَى)" (Muslim, Abū Dāwud, Nasā'ī)[5] or "he would place his hands on his knees (وَضَعَ يَدَيْهِ عَلَى رُكْبَتَيْهِ)." (Muslim, Ibn Mājah, Tirmidhī)[6]

One way to reconcile these two would be to place the hands on the thighs with the fingers on or near the knees.

- **Arms bent at the elbows**: The arms should not be held straight like an arrow but be in a relaxed position, which would make them slightly bent with the elbows pointing towards the thighs but not touching them. This is indicated from a ḥadīth that mention that he (s) "edged his right elbow on his right thigh (وَحَدَّ مِرْفَقَهُ الأَيْمَنَ عَلَى فَخِذِهِ الْيُمْنَى)." (Abū Dāwud, Nasāʾī)[7]
- **Fingers kept in a natural state**: We found no narration on whether the fingers should be closed together or separated. That being the case, it seems that fingers should be kept in their natural, relaxed state – neither spreading them wide or sticking them close together by force.

- **Scholars' opinions**: According to the Ḥanafī and Shāfiʿī schools, the left and the right foot should be kept as concluded above. The Mālikī school also recommends a similar sitting.[8] As for where to keep the hands, the Mālikī school recommends that the hands be on the thighs near the knees. According to the Shāfiʿī school, the fingertips should be on the knees, which would also make the hands on the thighs but near the knees.[9]
- For the complete list of ḥadīths and detailed discussion on this, see *Manner of the First Sitting* on page 332 in the main book.

Figure 8: The First Sitting (Iftirāsh)

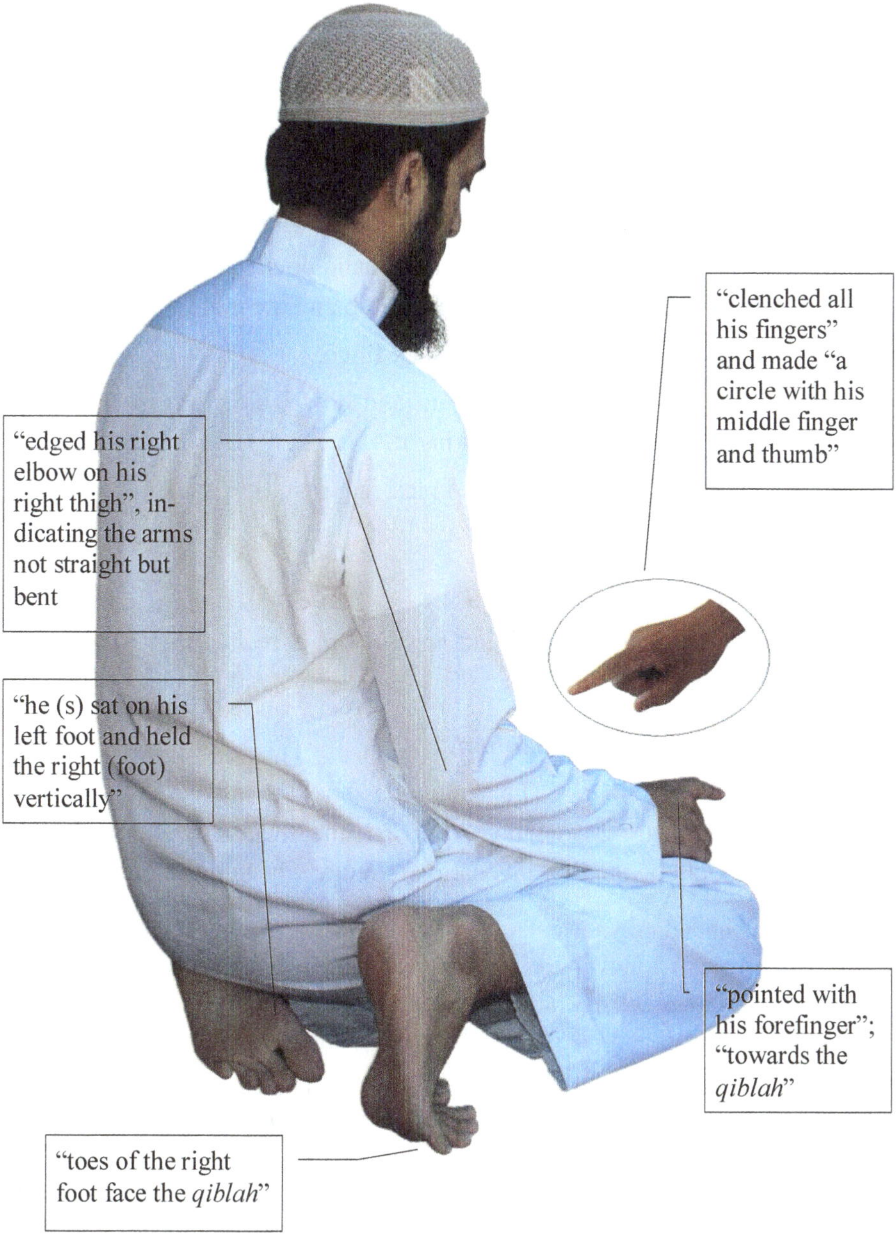

Ḥadīths and discussion about the position of the index and the other fingers appear on page 120 below.

<u>Incorrect practices, or practices that do not have any textual evidence</u>

- Leaning the body forward (instead, one should sit upright and be relaxed).
- Crisscrossing the feet and sitting on both of them.
- Keeping the arms straight, without bending at the elbows.
- Keeping the fingers of the right hand open (i.e., not closing them and making a circle with the thumb and the middle finger).
- Purposefully bending the index finger.
- Moving the index finger up and down, sideways, in a circular motion, or constantly jerking it.
- Raising and lowering the index finger at a particular point during the *tashahhud*.

Recitation in the First Sitting

During the first and the final sitting, a *dhikr* is recited that is known as the *tashahhud*.

When to Recite the *Tashahhud*

- **In every sitting**: The *tashahhud* should be recited in the ṣalāh at every sitting, i.e., both the first and the final sitting. Also, it should be the first invocation to recite when one sits in the ṣalāh.

> ʿAbdullāh ibn Masʿūd (r) narrated: ... [the Prophet (s)] said, "When you sit following every two *rakʿahs* (إِذَا قَعَدْتُمْ فِي كُلِّ رَكْعَتَيْنِ), then say *at-taḥiyyātu lillāhi* ..." (Nasāʾī, Tirmidhī)[10]

> Abū Mūsā al-Ashʿarī (r) narrated: ... The Messenger of Allāh (s) addressed us and explained our Sunnah to us and taught us our ṣalāh. He said, "... when he sits (in the ṣalāh) (وَإِذَا كَانَ عِنْدَ الْقَعْدَةِ), let the first thing one of you says (مِنْ أَوَّلِ قَوْلِ) be *at-taḥiyyātut-ṭ-ṭayyibātu-ṣ-ṣalawātu lillāhi* ..." (Muslim, Ibn Mājah, Abū Dāwud, Nasāʾī)[11]

- **Scholars' opinions**: Scholars agree that the Prophetic example is to recite the *tashahhud* in both the first and the final sitting.[12]
- For further evidence and discussion on this, see *When to Recite the Tashahhud* on page 343 in the main book.

Text of the *Tashahhud*

- **Several texts**: There are several forms of the *tashahhud* that the Messenger of Allāh (s) used to recite during the first and the final sitting. The *tashahhud* that is supported by most narrations is the following by Ibn Mas'ūd (r):

  التحياتُ للهِ والصلواتُ والطيباتُ، السلامُ عليكَ أيُّها النبيُّ ورحمةُ الله وبركاتُه، السلامُ علينا وعلى عبادِ اللهِ الصالحين، أشهدُ أن لا إلهَ إلا الله وأشهدُ أن محمدًا عبدُه ورسولُه

  All the compliments, prayers, and good words are due to Allāh. Peace be upon you O Prophet, and Allāh's Mercy and Blessings. Peace be upon us and on the righteous slaves of Allāh. I bear witness that there is no one worthy of worship except Allāh and I bear witness that Muḥammad is His slave and Messenger. (Bukhārī, Muslim, Abū Dāwud, Nasā'ī, Ibn Mājah, Tirmidhī)[13]

- **Scholars' opinions**: According to most of the ḥadīth scholars, including Imām Muslim and Imām Tirmidhī, the *tashahhud* of Ibn Mas'ūd (r) is the most authentic. This *tashahhud* is used by the Ḥanafī school. It is also preferred by scholars such as An-Nawawī, Ibn Ḥajar, and Imām Aḥmad.[14]
- For other versions of the *tashahhud* and the supporting ḥadīths, see *Text of the Tashahhud* on page 339 in the main book.

Recitations During Sittings Are to Be Done Quietly

- **Reciting quietly**: Recitation of the *tashahhud* during the sittings is to be done quietly.

ʿAbdullāh ibn Masʿūd (r) said, "It is from the Sunnah to recite the *tashahhud* quietly (مِنَ السُّنَّةِ أَنْ يُخْفَى التَّشَهُّدِ)." (Abū Dāwud, Tirmidhī)[15]

- **Scholars' opinions**: Scholars unanimously agree that all recitations in the first and final sitting position are to be done quietly.[16]

Raising the Index Finger (الإشارة بالسبابة)

- There are many ḥadīths that describe how the Messenger of Allāh (s) raised his index finger and how he maintained the other fingers. These ḥadīths show the following details:
  - **Index finger raised, others stay closed**: He (s) "clenched all his fingers (وَقَبَضَ أَصَابِعَهُ كُلَّهَا) and pointed with the finger (وَأَشَارَ بِإِصْبَعِهِ) that is next to the thumb (الَّتِي تَلِي الإِبْهَامَ)." (Muslim, Abū Dāwud, Nasāʾī)[17]. This shows that only the index finger is raised while the other fingers stay closed or clenched. (For a detailed discussion on this, see *Which Finger to Raise* on page 351 in the main book.)
  - **Naturally raised, not willfully bent or straightened**: There is one *ḥasan* ḥadīth that mentions that the Messenger of Allāh (s) raised his index finger "(curving it) downwards slightly (قَدْ حَنَّاهَا شَيْئًا)." (Nasāʾī, Abū Dāwud)[18]. There is, however, no authentic ḥadīth in support of bending the index finger in the *Six Most Authentic Books* although there are many narrations available on raising the index finger. In its natural state – when it is raised – the index finger is not straight like an arrow but is slightly curved. It is likely that this is what is meant by this *ḥasan* ḥadīth. That being the case, the index finger should be in a natural and relaxed state – one should neither bend it willfully nor stiffen it in order to keep it perfectly straight. (For a detailed discussion on this, see *To Bend or Not to Bend the Finger* on page 352 in the main book.)

- **Circle with the thumb and the middle finger**: When he (s) raised the index finger, he "placed the thumb on the middle finger (وَوَضَعَ إِبْهَامَهُ عَلَى إِصْبَعِهِ الوُسْطَى)," (Muslim)[19] thereby "making a circle with his thumb and the middle finger (حَلَّقَ الإِبْهَامَ وَالوُسْطَى)." (Ibn Mājah)[20] (For a detailed discussion on this, see *Forming Circle with the Thumb and the Middle Finger* on page 352 in the main book.)

- **Not moving the finger**: In regards to moving the finger, one Companion (r) narrated, "I saw him moving it (يُحَرِّكُهَا)" (Nasā'ī)[21]. This is the only narration among more than thirty narrations available on this subject that mentioned this moving. When one raises the finger and keep it raised for more than a few seconds, it can sometimes slightly shake, especially if he is weak or tired. This occasionally happens to people who are middle aged or older. Such involuntary shaking of the finger may be what gave the impression in this one particular narration of Wā'il bin Ḥujr (s) that the finger was moving. In any case, this narration is contradicted by another narration by ʿAbdullāh ibn az-Zubair (r) who reported, "he would not move it (وَلاَ يُحَرِّكُهَا)" (Abū Dāwud, *ḥasan*).[22] Furthermore, the same exact ḥadīth of Wā'il bin Ḥujr (r) is also narrated in ḥadīth no. 1266 in Nasā'ī and ḥadīth no. 726 in Abū Dāwud, both of them *ṣaḥīḥ*. Yet, none of these other two texts mentions that the finger was moving, although all three of these narrations came through the same *tābiʿ* – ʿĀṣim bin Kulaib. So, there is evidence for both, but evidence for not moving it seems stronger. (For a detailed discussion on this, see *Whether the Finger Should Be Moved* on page 353 in the main book.)

- **When to raise/lower the finger**: The Messenger of Allāh (s) "would place his hands on his knees, then point with his finger (ثُمَّ أَشَارَ بِإِصْبَعِهِ)" (Nasā'ī)[23], thus indicating that the index finger should be raised immediately upon sitting. As for when to lower it, there is no direct text on this. However, a number of narrations mention that he (s) raised the finger "*during the tashahhud* (فِي التَّشَهُّدِ)" (Muslim, Nasā'ī, Ibn Mājah)[24], which suggests that it should stay raised throughout the sitting. (For a detailed discussion on this, see *When to Raise and Lower the Finger* on page 356 in the main book.)

- **Where to look**: Throughout the sitting, one should keep focus at the place of *sajdah* since "his gaze did not go beyond his pointing (لا يُجَاوِزُ بَصَرُهُ إِشَارَتَهُ)" (Nasā'ī)[25], if it is interpreted to be what the finger was pointing at. There is also a narration that mentions that "he would look at it or thereabouts (رَمَى بِبَصَرِهِ إِلَيْهَا أَوْ نَحْوِهَا)" (Nasā'ī)[26], which shows that one may look at the raised finger from time to time. (For a detailed discussion on this, see *Looking at the Finger or What It Points At* on page 354 in the main book.)

- For the complete texts of all the ḥadīths and detailed discussions, including opinions of the scholars, on these points, see the section *Raising the Index Finger* on page 348 in the main book.

Rising from the First Sitting

After the first sitting, the Messenger of Allāh (s) would stand up, and as he did so, he would say the *takbīr* and raise his hands.

Saying the *Takbīr* when Standing up from the First Sitting

- ***Takbīr* when standing up**: As the Messenger of Allāh (s) rose from the first sitting, he would say the *takbīr*.

> Abū Ḥumaid as-Sā'idī (r) observed the ṣalāh of the Messenger of Allāh (s) and narrated: "... When he stood up after two *rak'ahs* (إذا قام من الركعتين), he would say the *takbīr* and raise his hands (كبر ورفع يديه) to the level of his shoulders." (Abū Dāwud, Ibn Mājah)[27]

- For the full text of this ḥadīth as well as additional ḥadīths on this, see *Takbīr when Standing up from the First Sitting* on page 208 in the main book.

Raising the Hands when Standing up from the First Sitting

- **Hands to be raised**: When the Messenger of Allāh (s) stood up from the first sitting, he would raise his hands. This is shown in the ḥadīth of Abū Ḥumaid as-Sāʿidī (r) above.

- **Scholars' opinions**: According to the Shāfiʿī school, it is from the Sunnah of the Prophet (s) to raise the hands when standing up for the third *rakʿah* after the first sitting.[28]

- For additional ḥadīths on this, see *Raising the Hands when Standing up from the First Sitting* on page 213 in the main book.

---

[1] Muslim, *Ṣalāh*, 1110; Abū Dāwud, *Ṣalāh*, 783.

[2] Bukhārī, *Adhān*, 828; Abū Dāwud, *Ṣalāh*, 964.

[3] Muslim, *Ṣalāh*, 1110; Bukhārī, *Adhān*, 828; Abū Dāwud, *Ṣalāh*, 783.

[4] Abū Dāwud, *Ṣalāh*, 967.

[5] Muslim, *Masājid*, 1311-12; Abū Dāwud, *Ṣalāh*, 987; Nasā'ī, *Forgetfulness*, 1268, 1270.

[6] Muslim, *Masājid*, 1309-10; Ibn Mājah, *Establishing Ṣalāh*, 913; Tirmidhī, *Ṣalāh*, 294.

[7] Abū Dāwud, *Ṣalāh*, 726; Nasā'ī, *Commencement of Ṣalāh*, 890; *Forgetfulness*, 1266.

[8] Al-Jazīrī, *Islamic Jurisprudence*, pp. 316, 322, 342, 348.

[9] *Ibid.*, pp. 322, 342, 348.

[10] Nasā'ī, *At-Taṭbīq*, 1164, 1163, 1167; *Forgetfulness*, 1280; Tirmidhī, *Ṣalāh*, 289.

[11] Muslim, *Ṣalāh*, 904; Ibn Mājah, *Establishing Ṣalāh*, 901; Abū Dāwud, *Ṣalāh*, 972, 973; Nasā'ī, *Forgetfulness*, 1281; *At-Taṭbīq*, 1173, 1065, 1174.

[12] Al-Jazīrī, *Islamic Jurisprudence*, pp. 306-07, 317, 323.

[13] Bukhārī, *Adhān*, 831, 835; *Actions in Ṣalāh*, 1202; *Invocations*, 6328; *Tauḥīd*, 7381; Muslim, *Ṣalāh*, 897-00; Abū Dāwud, *Ṣalāh*, 968-69; Nasā'ī, *At-Taṭbīq*,

1164, 1163, 1167; *Forgetfulness*, 1278, 1280, 1299; Ibn Mājah, *Establishing Ṣalāh*, 899; Tirmidhī, *Ṣalāh*, 289.

[14] Sabiq, *Fiqh*, vol. 1, p. 125; Al-Jazīrī, *Islamic Jurisprudence*, pp. 306-07; Editor's commentary on Tirmidhī, *Ṣalāh*, 289-90.

[15] Abū Dāwud, *Ṣalāh*, 986; Tirmidhī, *Ṣalāh*, 291.

[16] Editor's commentary on Tirmidhī, *Ṣalāh*, 291.

[17] Muslim, *Masājid*, 1311, 1312; Nasā'ī, *Forgetfulness*, 1268; Abū Dāwud, *Ṣalāh*, 987.

[18] Nasā'ī, *Forgetfulness*, 1275; Abū Dāwud, *Ṣalāh*, 991, both graded *ḥasan*.

[19] Muslim, *Masājid*, 1308.

[20] Ibn Mājah, *Establishing Ṣalāh*, 912.

[21] Nasā'ī, *Commencement of Ṣalāh*, 890.

[22] Abū Dāwud, *Ṣalāh*, 990, graded *ḥasan*. Initial part of this narration comes from narration 989, which is referenced by narration 990.

[23] Nasā'ī, *At-Taṭbīq*, 1162.

[24] Muslim, *Masājid*, 1310; Nasā'ī, *Forgetfulness*, 1276; Ibn Mājah, *Establishing Ṣalāh*, 912.

[25] Nasā'ī, *Forgetfulness*, 1276.

[26] Nasā'ī, *At-Taṭbīq*, 1161.

[27] Abū Dāwud, *Ṣalāh*, 730; Ibn Mājah, *Establishing Ṣalāh*, 862, 1061.

[28] Al-Misrī, *Reliance of the Traveller*, p. 141; Al-Jazīrī, *Islamic Jurisprudence*, p. 324.

The Final Sitting (الجلوس الأخير)

The final sitting is the sitting in which ṣalāh is concluded with the *taslīm*. This would be the first and the only sitting in a two-*rak'ah* ṣalāh, and the second sitting in a three or four-*rak'ah* ṣalāh.

Manner of the Final Sitting (التورك)

- **Elements of the *tawarruk***: In the final sitting, the Messenger of Allāh (s) used to sit in *tawarruk* fashion, which is nearly the same as the *iftirāsh* position (see *Manner of the First Sitting* on page 115 above) except that he would:
    - Extend his left leg further and make it come out from under his right leg.
    - This would make both legs to be on the right side, and
    - Place the left posterior on the ground, making one sitting on it.
- **Evidence**: These postures are evident from the following ḥadīths:
    - "in the last *rak'ah*, he pushed his left foot forward (قدَّم رجْلَه اليُسْرَى) and kept the other foot held upright (ونَصَبَ الأخْرَى) and sat over his posteriors (وقَعَدَ علَى مقْعدَتِهِ)." (Bukhārī)[1]
    - "if it were the 4th (*rak'ah*), he allowed his left buttock to touch the ground (أفْضَ بِورَكِهِ اليُسْرَى إلَى الأرْضِ), and stuck both

his legs out on one side (the right side) (وَأخْرَجَ قدَمَيْهِ مِنْ نَاحِيَةٍ وَاحِدَةٍ)." (Abū Dāwud)[2]

- "when he performed the *sajdah* that is before the *taslīm*, he would move his left leg further (أخَّرَ رِجْلَهُ الْيُسْرَى) and sit on his buttocks on his left side *mutawarrikan* way (وقَعَدَ مُتَوَرِّكًا عَلَى شِقِّهِ الأيْسَرِ) …" (Abū Dāwud, Tirmidhī, Ibn Mājah)[3]
- "At the end of the last two *rak'ahs* of the ṣalāh, the Prophet (s) would move his left leg further (أخَّرَ رِجْلَهُ الْيُسْرَى) and sit on his (left) buttock, *mutawarrikan* way (وقَعَدَ عَلَى شِقِّهِ مُتَوَرِّكًا), then he would say the *taslīm*." (Nasā'ī)[4]

- **Scholars' opinions**: Imām Shāfi'ī's opinion is the same as what is concluded above, i.e., one should sit *iftirāsh* in the first sitting and sit *tawarruk* in the final sitting, including the sitting in two-*rak'ah* prayers.[5] Imām Mālik, holds it "recommended" to sit *tawarruk* in both middle and final sitting. Imām Abū Ḥanīfah 's opinion is to sit *iftirāsh* in both the first and final sittings.[6] Imām Aḥmad's opinion is the same as Imām Shāfi'ī, with the exception that in a two *rak'ahs* ṣalāh, one should sit *iftirāsh*, not *tawarruk*; so, *tawarruk* sitting is to be done in the final sitting only when the ṣalāh has two sittings.[7] This is also the view of Al-Albānī.[8]
- For additional ḥadīths and full discussion on this, see *Manner of the Final Sitting* on page 361 in the main book.
- **Not required**: It should be mentioned here that the *tawarruk* posture in the final sitting is not a required part of the ṣalāh. Although it is more rewarding to practice this posture in the final sitting since it is the prophetic example, one may use other valid options if it is painful and thus compromises one's concentration in ṣalāh. An evidence for this flexibility has been mentioned in *Avoiding Pains and Keeping the Right Priorities* on page 17.

Figure 9: The Final Sitting (Tawarruk)

Except for extending the left leg to come out from under the right shin, this sitting is nearly the same way as the *iftirāsh* sitting (see *Figure 8* on page 117).

<u>Incorrect practices, or practices that do not have any textual evidence</u>

- See the incorrect practices mentioned on page 117 (*Figure 8*).

Arguments Against the *Tawarruk* Sitting

According to the Ḥanafī school, one should always sit in *iftirāsh* fashion in the ṣalāh, whether in the first or the final sitting. The major arguments in support of this view have been fully examined in the section *Arguments Against the Tawarruk Sitting* on page 365 in the main book.

Recitations in the Final Sitting

- **What is recited in the final sitting**: During the final sitting of the ṣalāh, one should recite the following:
    - The *tashahhud.*
    - The invocation for sending ṣalāh on the Prophet (s).
    - The invocation for seeking refuge in Allāh (swt), and
    - Finally, the *taslīm* to the right and the left.
- **Personal *du'ā'***: Additionally, before the *taslīm*, one may add other invocations mentioned in the ḥadīth or make his own personal invocations.
- **Scholars' opinions**: According to the Ḥanafī, Shāfi'ī, and Ḥanbalī schools, reciting the *tashahhud* is obligatory, while the Mālikī school considers it a Sunnah.[9] Sending ṣalāh on the Prophet (s) is obligatory in the Shāfi'ī school and Sunnah in the other three schools.[10] According to the Ḥanafī school, it is Sunnah to recite *du'ā's* from the Qur'ān/ḥadīth.[11] As for the *taslīm*, it is required in the Shāfi'ī and the Ḥanbalī schools.[12]

The *Tashahhud*

- ***Tashahhud* in the final sitting**: As he did in the first sitting, the Prophet (s) would recite the *tashahhud* in the final sitting as well.

> 'Abdullāh ibn Mas'ūd (r) narrated: ... [the Prophet (s)] said, "When you sit following every two *rak'ahs* (إِذَا قَعَدْتُمْ فِي كُلِّ رَكْعَتَيْنِ), then say *at-taḥiyyātu lillāhi* ..." (Nasā'ī, Tirmidhī)[13]
>
> One of the narrations in Nasā'ī (no. 1167) includes the words "every time you sit." (فِي كُلِّ جَلْسَةٍ).

- For more ḥadīths on this, see *When to Recite the Tashahhud* on page 343 in the main book. For the wordings of this *dhikr*, see *Text of the Tashahhud* on page 119 above.

Sending Ṣalāh upon the Prophet

- **Only in the final sitting**: After the *tashahhud*, the Companions were urged to send ṣalāh on the Messenger of Allāh (s) and seek refuge in Allāh from a number of things before concluding the ṣalāh with the *taslīm*. As evident from the ḥadīth below, these were recited only in the final sitting.

> Abū Hurairah (r) narrated: The Messenger of Allāh (s) said, "When one of you has finished the final *tashahhud* (إِذَا فَرَغَ أَحَدُكُمْ مِنَ التَّشَهُّدِ الآخِرِ), let him seek refuge with Allāh from four things ..." (Muslim, Abū Dāwud, Ibn Mājah)[14]

- For further evidence and discussion on this, see *When to Recite Du'ā's for Sending Ṣalāh and Seeking Refuge* on page 385 in the main book.

Importance of Sending Ṣalāh upon the Prophet

- **Duty upon all believers**: It is an important duty upon the believers to send ṣalāh upon the Messenger of Allāh (s). Indeed, Allāh (swt) has commanded the believers to do so:

إِنَّ اللَّهَ وَمَلَائِكَتَهُ يُصَلُّونَ عَلَى النَّبِيِّ يَا أَيُّهَا الَّذِينَ آمَنُوا صَلُّوا عَلَيْهِ وَسَلِّمُوا تَسْلِيمًا

> Allāh and His angels send ṣalāh on the Prophet: O you who believe! Send ṣalāh on him, and offer *salām* to him with all respect. (33:56)

- **He (s) taught how to send ṣalāh**: When this command came, the Companions (r) asked the Prophet (s) regarding how to send ṣalāh on him. In response, he (s) taught them what to say when sending ṣalāh on him. For the ḥadīths on this, see *Importance of*

Sending Ṣalāh and Salām upon the Prophet on page 372 in the main book.

Text for Sending Ṣalāh upon the Prophet

- **Option for multiple *adhkār***: There are several texts available in the ḥadīth for sending ṣalāh on the Prophet (s), some of which are mentioned below. The texts in no. 1a and no. 1b are nearly identical and together have more narrations available than for any other ones.

(1a)

اللهمَّ صلِّ على محمدٍ وعلى آلِ محمدٍ ، كما صلَّيتَ على إبراهيمَ ، وعلى آلِ إبراهيمَ ، إنكَ حميدٌ مجيدٌ ، اللهمَّ بارِكْ على محمدٍ وعلى آلِ محمدٍ ، كما باركتَ على إبراهيمَ وعلى آلِ إبراهيمَ ، إنكَ حميدٌ مجيدٌ

O Allāh, send ṣalāh upon Muḥammad and the family of Muḥammad, as You sent ṣalāh upon Ibrāhīm and the family of Ibrāhīm. You are indeed Worthy of Praise, Full of Glory. O Allāh, send blessings upon Muḥammad and the family of Muḥammad, as You sent blessings upon Ibrāhīm and the family of Ibrāhīm. Indeed, You are the Praiseworthy, the Most Glorious. (Bukhārī, Nasā'ī)[15]

(1b)

اللهمَّ صلِّ على محمدٍ وعلى آلِ محمدٍ ، كما صلَّيتَ على آلِ إبراهيمَ ، إنك حَميدٌ مَجيدٌ ، اللهمَّ بارِكْ على محمدٍ وعلى آلِ محمدٍ ، كما بارَكتَ على آلِ إبراهيمَ ، إنك حَميدٌ مَجيدٌ

O Allāh, send ṣalāh upon Muḥammad and the family of Muḥammad, as You sent ṣalāh upon the family of Ibrāhīm. Indeed, You are the Praiseworthy, the Most Glorious. O Allāh, send blessings upon Muḥammad and the family of Muḥammad, as You sent blessings upon the family of Ibrāhīm. Indeed, You are the Praiseworthy, the Most Glorious. (Bukhārī, Muslim, Nasā'ī)[16]

(2)

اللهم صل على محمد وعلى آل محمد كما صليت على آل إبراهيم ، و بارك على محمد وآل محمد كما باركت على آل إبراهيم ، إنك حميد مجيد

O Allāh, send ṣalāh upon Muḥammad and the family of Muḥammad, as You sent ṣalāh upon the family of Ibrāhīm. And send blessings upon Muḥammad and the family of Muḥammad, as you sent blessings upon the family of Ibrāhīm. Indeed, You are the Praiseworthy, the Most Glorious. (Abū Dāwud)[17]

(3)

اللهم صل على محمد وعلى آل محمد كما صليت على آل إبراهيم ، و بارك على محمد وعلى آل محمد كما باركت على آل إبراهيم في العالمين ، إنك حميد مجيد

O Allāh, send ṣalāh upon Muḥammad and upon the family of Muḥammad, as You sent ṣalāh upon the family of Ibrāhīm. And send blessings upon Muḥammad and the family of Muḥammad, as you sent blessings upon the family of Ibrāhīm among the nations. Indeed, You are the Praiseworthy, the Most Glorious. (Muslim, Nasā'ī, Abū Dāwud, Tirmidhī)[18]

- **Scholars' opinions**: The text preferred by the Ḥanafī and the Mālikī schools is similar to no. 1a with these minor differences: it uses the phrase *innaka ḥamīdun majīd* once only at the end and adds *fil-ʿālamīna* before it.[19]
- For the other texts and the supporting ḥadīths, see *Text for Sending Ṣalāh upon the Prophet* on page 373 in the main book.

Seeking Refuge in Allāh

- **Seeking refuge from four things**: In the final sitting during the ṣalāh, the Prophet (s) used to seek refuge in Allāh (swt) from a number of things and also urged his Companions to do so. These are:

- From Hellfire.
- From the punishment in the grave.
- From trials and tribulations in life and at death, and
- From the trials of the Dajjāl

> Abū Hurairah (r) narrated: The Messenger of Allāh (s) said, "When one of you has finished the final *tashahhud* (إِذَا فَرَغَ أَحَدُكُمْ مِنَ التَّشَهُّدِ الآخِرِ), let him seek refuge with Allāh from four things (فَلْيَتَعَوَّذْ بِاللهِ مِنْ أَرْبَعٍ): from the punishment of Hell, from the punishment of the grave, from the trials of life and death, and from the evil of the Dajjāl." (Muslim, Abū Dāwud, Ibn Mājah, Nasā'ī)[20]

- For additional ḥadīths about the importance of seeking refuge in Allāh, see *Importance of Seeking Refuge* on page 380 in the main book.

Text for Seeking Refuge in Allāh

- **Several texts**: There are several forms of this *du'ā'* available in the books of ḥadīth, a few of which are mentioned below. The texts in no. 1 and no. 2 are nearly identical and together have more narrations available than for any other texts.

(1)

اللهم إني أعوذُ بك من عذابِ جهنمَ ، ومن عذابِ القبرِ ، ومن فتنةِ المحيا والمماتِ ، ومن شرِّ فتنةِ المسيحِ الدجالِ

O Allāh, I seek refuge in You from the punishment of Hell, and from the punishment of the grave, and from the trials of life and death, and form the evil of the tribulation of the Dajjāl.
(Muslim, Abū Dāwud, Ibn Mājah, Nasā'ī)[21]

(2)

اللهم إني أعوذ بك من عذاب جهنم ، وأعوذ بك من عذاب القبر ، وأعوذ بك من فتنة الدجال ، وأعوذ بك من فتنة المحيا والممات

O Allāh, I seek refuge in You from the punishment of Hell, and I seek refuge in you from the punishment of the grave, and I seek refuge in you from the tribulation of the Dajjāl, and I seek refuge in you from the trials of life and death. (Abū Dāwud)[22]

(3)

اللهم إني أعوذ بك من عذاب القبر ، وأعوذ بك من فتنة المسيح الدجال ، وأعوذ بك من فتنة المحيا والممات ، اللهم إني أعوذ بك من المأثم والمغرم

O Allāh, I seek refuge in You from the punishment of the grave, and from the trials of Masīḥ Dajjāl, and I seek refuge in You from the trials of life and trials of death. O Allāh, I seek refuge in You from sins and form being in debt. (Muslim, Bukhārī, Nasā'ī, Abū Dāwud)[23]

- **Scholars' opinions**: According to the Ḥanbalī school, the Prophetic Sunnah is to recite the text in no. 1.[24]
- For the additional texts and the supporting ḥadīths, see *Text for Seeking Refuge* on page 382 in the main book.

Other *Du'ā's* from the Sunnah

- **Other *Du'ā's***: Besides the above standard invocations for sending ṣalāh on the Prophet (s) and seeking refuge in Allāh (swt), the books of ḥadīth mention additional *du'ā's* that the Prophet (s) either occasionally recited during the ṣalāh or asked the Companions (r) to recite. Some of these are mentioned below.

(1)

اللهم إني ظلَمتُ نفسي ظلمًا كثيرًا، ولا يَغفِرُ الذُّنوبَ إلا أنتَ، فاغفِرْ لي مَغفِرَةً من عِندِك، وارحَمْني، إنك أنت الغفورُ الرحيمُ

O Allāh, verily I have wronged myself much, and no one except You forgives sins, so grant me forgiveness from You, and have mercy on me, You are indeed the Oft-Forgiver, the Most Merciful. (Bukhārī, Muslim, Ibn Mājah, Tirmidhī, Nasā'ī)[25]

(2)

اللهم اغفر لي ما قدمت وما أخرت ، وما أسررت وما أعلنت ، وما أسرفت ، وما أنت أعلم به مني ، أنت المقدم وأنت المؤخر ، لا إله إلا أنت

O Allāh, forgive me for what I have done and what I have yet to do, and what I have done in private and what I have done in open, and my transgression, and all that You know from me. You are the One Who advances (whom You will), and You are the One Who moves back (whom You will), there is no deity worthy of worship except You. (Muslim, Tirmidhī)[26]

(3)

اللهم إني أعوذ بك من شر ما عملت ومن شر ما لم أعمل

O Allāh, I seek refuge with You from the evil of what I have done and the evil of what I have not done. (Nasā'ī)[27]

- **Scholars' opinions**: According to the Shāfi'ī school, it is Sunnah to make *du'ā'* before the *taslīm*, and one may ask for anything that is good for his faith or his worldly existence. The best practice, however, is to use the *du'ā's* that are in the ḥadīth. The Ḥanbalī school also has similar views. The Ḥanafī school holds that the Prophetic example is to make *du'ā'* in the final sitting from the Qur'ān or the ḥadīth only. According to the Mālikī school, it is "recommended" to make *du'ā'* in the final sitting after sending ṣalāh on the Prophet (s) asking for anything, whether in this world or the Next, but it is preferable to make certain specific *du'ā's* from the Sunnah.[28]
- For additional *du'ā's* and the supporting ḥadīths, see *Other Du'ā's from the Sunnah* on page 387 in the main book.

Making Personal *Du'ā'*

- **Making *Du'ā'***: After reciting the *tashahhud*, sending ṣalāh on the Prophet (s), seeking refuge in Allāh, and reciting any other *du'ā's* that are mentioned in the ḥadīth, one may also make personal supplication to Allāh (swt) seeking what he wants.

> Abū Hurairah (r) narrated: The Messenger of Allāh (s) said, "When one of you recites the *tashahhud*, let him seek refuge with Allāh from four things: from the torment of Hell, from the torment of the grave, from the trials of life and death, and from the evil of the Dajjāl. Then let him pray for himself asking whatever he wants (ثُمَّ يَدْعُو لِنَفْسِهِ بِمَا بَدَا لَهُ)." (Nasā'ī)[29]

- **Personal words**: One may use his own choice of words in expressing his desire to Allāh (swt).

> ʿAbdullāh ibn Masʿūd (r) narrated: The Messenger of Allāh (s) said, "... when anyone of you sits (during the ṣalāh), let him say *at-taḥiyyātu lillāhi wa-ṣ-ṣalawātu wa-ṭ-ṭayyibātu* ... Then after that, let him choose (ثُمَّ لْيَتَخَيَّرْ بَعْدُ ذَلِكَ) whatever words he wants" (مِنَ الْكَلَامِ مَا شَاءَ). (Nasā'ī)[30]

- **Scholars' opinions**: According to the Mālikī, Shāfiʿī, and the Ḥanbalī schools, one may make personal *duʿā'* at the end of the final sitting using his own words, although it is preferable to use the *duʿā's* that are in the Sunnah.[31]

- For more ḥadīths and discussion on this, see *Making Personal Duʿā'* on page 389 in the main book.

---

[1] Bukhārī, *Adhān*, 828.

[2] Abū Dāwud, *Ṣalāh*, 731-32, 965.

[3] Abū Dāwud, *Ṣalāh*, 730, 963; Tirmidhī, *Ṣalāh*, 304-05; Ibn Mājah, *Establishing Ṣalāh*, 1061.

[4] Nasā'ī, *Forgetfulness*, 1263.

[5] Editor's commentary on Tirmidhī, *Ṣalāh*, 293; Al-Jazīrī, *Islamic Jurisprudence*, p. 342.

[6] Al-Misrī, *Reliance of the Traveller*, p. 142; Al-Jazīrī, *Islamic Jurisprudence*, p. 316, 342, 348; Editor's commentary on Tirmidhī, *Ṣalāh*, 293. The Mālikī school also holds that the right foot should be vertical and the underside of the right big toe should be on the floor. (Al-Jazīrī, *Islamic Jurisprudence*, p 348.)

[7] Editor's commentary on Tirmidhī, *Ṣalāh*, 293; Al-Jazīrī, *Islamic Jurisprudence*, pp. 323, 342-43.

[8] Al-Albānī, *The Prophet's Prayer Described*, pp. 65, 85.

[9] Al-Jazīrī, *Islamic Jurisprudence*, pp. 305-07.

[10] *Ibid.*, pp. 306, 345.

[11] *Ibid.*, p. 316.

[12] *Ibid.*, p. 306.

[13] Nasā'ī, *At-Taṭbīq*, 1164, 1163, 1167; *Forgetfulness*, 1280; Tirmidhī, *Ṣalāh*, 289.

[14] Muslim, *Masājid*, 1326; Abū Dāwud, *Ṣalāh*, 983; Ibn Mājah, *Establishing Ṣalāh*, 909.

[15] Bukhārī, *Stories of the Prophets*, 3370; Nasā'ī, *Forgetfulness*, 1289.

[16] Bukhārī, *Commentary*, 4797; *Invocations*, 6357; Muslim, *Ṣalāh*, 908-9; Nasā'ī, *Forgetfulness*, 1288, 1290.

[17] Abū Dāwud, *Ṣalāh*, 977.

[18] Muslim, *Ṣalāh*, 907; Nasā'ī, *Forgetfulness*, 1286; Abū Dāwud, *Ṣalāh*, 980; Tirmidhī, *Tafsīr*, 3220.

[19] Al-Jazīrī, *Islamic Jurisprudence*, p. 345.

[20] Muslim, *Masājid*, 1326-27; Abū Dāwud, *Ṣalāh*, 983; Ibn Mājah, *Establishing Ṣalāh*, 909; Nasā'ī, *Forgetfulness*, 1311.

[21] Muslim, *Masājid*, 1324, 1326-27; Abū Dāwud, *Ṣalāh*, 983; Ibn Mājah, *Establishing Ṣalāh*, 909; Nasā'ī, *Forgetfulness*, 1311.

[22] Abū Dāwud, *Ṣalāh*, 984.

[23] Muslim, *Masājid*, 1325; Bukhārī, *Adhān*, 832; Nasā'ī, *Forgetfulness*, 1310; Abū Dāwud, *Ṣalāh*, 880.

[24] Al-Jazīrī, *Islamic Jurisprudence*, p. 346.

[25] Bukhārī, *Adhān*, 834; *Invocations*, 6326; Muslim, *Remembrance*, 6869-70; Ibn Mājah, *Supplication*, 3835; Tirmidhī, *Supplications*, 3531; Nasā'ī, *Forgetfulness*, 1303.

[26] Muslim, *Traveller's Prayer*, 1812; Tirmidhī, *Supplications*, 3421-22.

[27] Nasā'ī, *Forgetfulness*, 1308.

[28] Al-Jazīrī, *Islamic Jurisprudence*, pp. 345-46.

[29] Nasā'ī, *Forgetfulness*, 1311.

[30] Nasā'ī, *Forgetfulness*, 1280.

[31] Al-Jazīrī, *Islamic Jurisprudence*, pp. 345-46.

Ending the Ṣalāh

One ends the ṣalāh by uttering the *taslīm*, which is the greeting of peace. Thereafter, if he led the ṣalāh as an *imām*, then he turns around and faces the people. Following the example of the Prophet (s), he may also stay seated for a while and recite various *adhkar*.

The *Taslīm* (التسليم)

- **The final action in the ṣalāh**: The final action with which the ṣalāh is concluded is the *taslīm*. After the *taslīm*, the Prophet (s) entered into normal state, such as remaining sitting in ordinary and relaxed way, turning around, making *adhkār*, talking to the Companions, departing, etc.

> Umm Salāmah (r) narrated: "The Prophet (s) when he said the *taslīm* used to stay at his place for a while (كَانَ إِذَا سَلَّمَ يَمْكُثُ فِي مَكَانِهِ يَسِيرًا)." (Bukhārī)[1]

> ʿAlī ibn Abī Ṭālib (r) narrated: The Messenger of Allāh (s) said, "The key to ṣalāh is purification, and its sacredness (begins) with the *takbīr*, and its release is the *taslīm* (وَتَحْلِيلُهَا التَّسْلِيمُ)." (Abū Dāwud, *ḥasan*)[2]

- **Scholars' opinions**: The Mālikī, Shāfiʿī, and Ḥanbalī schools unanimously agree that the *taslīm* is the last action in the ṣalāh and it is required to terminate the ṣalāh. The Ḥanafī school also holds that the ṣalāh is concluded with the *taslīm*; it is, however, not required but a *wājib*.[3]

- For additional ḥadīths on this, see *The Taslīm* on page 396 in the main book.

Text of the *Taslīm*

- **Same text on both sides**: The text of the *taslīm* on both the right and the left side is *as-salāmu ʿalaikum wa raḥmatullāh* (السَّلَامُ عَلَيْكُمْ وَرَحْمَةُ اللَّهِ).

> ʿAbdullāh b. Masʿūd (r) narrated: "I saw the Messenger of Allāh (s) ... he said the *salām* on his right and his left [saying] *as-salāmu ʿalaikum wa raḥmatullāh* ..." (Nasāʾī)[4]

- **Same text in all *ṣaḥīḥ* narrations**: There are many *ṣaḥīḥ* narrations in the *Six Most Authentic Books* about what Messenger of Allāh (s) said in the *taslīm* and all of them mention this text.

- **Adding *wa barakātuh***: There is a single narration by Wā'il bin Ḥujr (r) which include the word *wa barakātuh* in the right-side *taslīm*. This, however, is a *ḥasan* narration, and, therefore, cannot supersede the overwhelming number of authentic narrations by multiple Companions (r) that mention that the text of the *taslīm* is *as-salāmu ʿalaikum wa raḥmatullāh* on both the right and the left sides.

- **Scholars' opinions**: According to the Ḥanbalī school, the proper text to terminate the ṣalāh is *as-salāmu ʿalaikum wa raḥmatullāh*. The Shāfiʿī school does not consider this exact text to be required, but preferable. The Mālikī school only requires the phrase *as-salāmu ʿalaikum*.[5]

- For more evidence and discussion on this, see *Manner of Making the Taslīm* on page 398 in the main book.

Turning Fully to the Right and the Left

- **Complete turn**: When saying the *taslīm*, one should turn his head completely to the right and to the left towards the people as if he is greeting them.

- **Cheeks fully visible from behind**: He should not turn his head only half way, neither should he look down at his shoulder, but turn his head fully and horizontally so that his cheek is aligned with and parallel to his shoulders, making them fully visible from behind.

> Sa'd bin Abī Waqqāṣ (r) narrated: I used to see the Messenger of Allāh (s) saying the *salām* to his right and to his left (عَنْ يمينِهِ وعَنْ يسارِهِ), until I could see the whiteness of his cheek (حَتَّى أرى بياضَ خدِّهِ). (Muslim, Nasā'ī)[6]

> 'Abdullāh b. Mas'ūd (r) narrated: The Messenger of Allāh (s) used to say the *salām* to his right (عَنْ يمينِهِ) so that the whiteness of his cheek could be seen (حَتَّى يَبْدُوَ بَيَاضُ خَدِّهِ), and to his left (وَعَنْ يَسَارِهِ) so that the whiteness of his cheek could be seen (حَتَّى يَبْدُوَ بَيَاضُ خَدِّهِ). (Nasā'ī)[7]

- **Scholars' opinions**: According to the Ḥanafī, Shāfi'ī, and the Ḥanbalī schools, the Prophetic example is to make the *taslīm* to the right and then to the left.[8]

- For more ḥadīths and discussion on this, see *How Much to Turn when Saying the Taslīm* on page 401 in the main book.

Figure 10: The Taslīm

Incorrect practices, or practices that do not have any textual evidence

- Looking down at the shoulders when making *taslīm*.
- Turning partially (less then fully over the shoulders).
- Turning too much and looking at the people behind over the shoulders.

Whom Do We Address when Saying the *Taslīm*

- **Addressing the believers**: When one says the *taslīm* at the end of the ṣalāh, he primarily addresses the believers on his right and left. This is evident from the Prophet's (s) instruction that one should "turn to his companions" and address the *salām* "to his brother, the one on his right and on his left."

Jābir bin Samurah (r) narrated: [The Prophet (s) said]: "... When any one of you says the *salām* (إذا سلَّمَ أحَدُكُمْ), let him turn to his companions (فَلْيَلْتَفِتْ إلى صاحِبِهِ) ..." (Nasā'ī)[9]

Jābir bin Samurah (r) narrated: [The Prophet (s) said]: "... it is sufficient for one of you to place his hand on his thigh, then say the *salām* to his brother, the one on his right and on his left (عَلَى أخيهِ مَنْ عَلَى يَمِينِهِ وشِمالِهِ)." (Muslim, Nasā'ī, Abū Dāwud)[10]

- **Scholars' opinions**: According to the Ḥanafī school, the *imām* addresses *salām* to those who prayed behind him, to the guardian angels, to the righteous *jinns* and unseen beings. For those who are led, they address the *imām* and others he prayed with. If praying alone, he addresses the angels only. The Shāfiʿī school holds that the greeting is done to the angels, to believing humans and *jinns*, including the *imām* and other fellow Muslims one prayed with. In the Mālikī school, when praying alone or being led in ṣalāh, then the intention is to both conclude the ṣalāh and greet the angels. If leading as *imām*, then the intention is to conclude the ṣalāh and to greet those he led.[11]
- For additional ḥadīths and a detailed discussion on this, see *Whom Do We Address when Saying the Taslīm* on page 402 in the main book.

Turning Around and Facing the People

- **Facing the people**: After ending the ṣalāh, the Messenger of Allāh (s) would turn around to face the Companions (r). Many narrations by multiple Companions (r) show that this was a regular practice of the Messenger of Allāh (s).

Samurah bin Jundub (r) narrated: "The Prophet (s) used to turn around to face us on completion of the ṣalāh (إذا صلَّى صلاةً أقْبَلَ عَلَيْنا بوَجْهِهِ)." (Bukhārī)[12]

> Zaid bin Khālid al-Juhanī (r) narrated: "The Prophet (s) led us in the Fajr ṣalāh at Ḥudaibiyah after a rainy night. On completion of the ṣalāh, he faced the people (فَلَمَّا انْصَرَفَ أَقْبَلَ عَلَى النَّاسِ) and said ..." (Bukhārī)[13]

- For more ḥadīths on this, see *Turning Around and Facing the People* on page 405 in the main book.

Facing the People at a Slight Angle

- **Facing people on the right**: It seems that when the Messenger of Allāh (s) turned around after the *taslīm*, he would face the people who stood on his right side, perhaps only by a small degree.

> Al-Barā' bin ʿĀzib (r) narrated: "We would prefer to pray on the right side (أَحْبَبْنَا أَنْ نَكُونَ عَنْ يَمِينِهِ) of the Messenger of Allāh (s) whenever we prayed, because he would then turn around to face us (فَيُقْبِلُ عَلَيْنَا بِوَجْهِهِ) ..." (Muslim, Abū Dāwud)[14]

- **Evidence for sitting at an angle**: In the above ḥadīth, Al-Barā' bin ʿĀzib (r) preferred to pray on the right side of the Messenger of Allāh (s), and the reason he provided for this was "because he would then turn around to face us." This indicates that when the Messenger of Allāh (s) turned around to face the people, he sat at a slight angle facing a little more to the left than to the right, meaning facing more towards those who stood on his right side than those on the left. And Allāh knows best.

Remaining Sitting for a While After the Ṣalāh

- **Usual practice**: It was the usual practice of the Messenger of Allāh (s) to remain sitting for a while after saying the *taslīm* at the end of the obligatory prayers. During this time, he would recite various *adhkār* and supplications.

> Umm Salāmah (r) narrated: "Whenever the Messenger of Allāh (s) completed the ṣalāh with *taslīm*, the women used to get up immediately and the Messenger of Allāh (s) would remain at his place for sometime (وَيَمْكُثُ هُوَ فِي مَقَامِهِ يَسِيرًا) before getting up (قَبْلَ أَنْ يَقُومَ) ..." (Bukhārī)[15]

- For more ḥadīths and discussion on this, see *Remaining Sitting for a While After the Compulsory Prayers* on page 407 in the main book.

Adhkār After Ending the Ṣalāh

فَإِذَا قَضَيْتُمُ الصَّلاَةَ فَاذْكُرُواْ اللّهَ قِيَامًا وَقُعُودًا وَعَلَى جُنُوبِكُمْ

And when you have finished your prayer, remember Allāh – standing and sitting and lying down on your sides. (4:103)

- **Option for multiple *adhkār***: The Messenger of Allāh (s) would recite various *adhkār* during the brief period of time he sat after he ended the ṣalāh and faced the people. A few of these with most supporting narrations are mentioned below.

(1)

سُبْحانَ الله (Glory to Allāh), 33 times

الحَمْدُ لِلَّه (All Praise is to Allāh), 33 times

الله أكْبر (Allāh is the Greatest), 33 or 34 times

(Bukhārī, Muslim, Nasā'ī, Ibn Mājah)[16]

(2)

سُبْحانَ الله، الحَمْدُ لِلَّه، الله أكْبر 33 times each, plus

لا إله إلا الله وَحْدَهُ لا شَرِيكَ لَهُ لَهُ المُلكُ ولَهُ الحَمْدُ وَهُوَ على كُلِّ شَيءٍ قَدِيرٌ

There is no one worthy of worship but Allāh, the One and Only, Who has no partners. His is the Dominion, and His is the Praise, and He has power over all things. (Muslim, Abū Dāwud)[17]

(3)

اسْتَغْفِرُ اللَّه ، اسْتَغْفِرُ اللَّه ، اسْتَغْفِرُ اللَّه

I ask Allāh for forgiveness, I ask Allāh for forgiveness, I ask Allāh for forgiveness. (Muslim, Nasā'ī, Abū Dāwud, Ibn Mājah, Tirmidhī)[18]

(4)

اللهمَّ أنت السلامُ ومنك السلامُ ، تباركت يا ذا الجلالِ والإكرامِ

O Allāh, You are the Peace, from You is all Peace; blessed are You, Possessor of Majesty and Honor.
(Muslim, Nasā'ī, Abū Dāwud, Ibn Mājah, Tirmidhī)[19]

- For a complete list of the *adhkār* and supporting ḥadīths, see *Adhkār After Ending the Ṣalāh* on page 408 in the main book.

Counting by the Fingers

When reciting certain *adhkār* a specific number of times, one may use his fingers for counting. This was done by the Messenger of Allāh (s) himself as mentioned in the following ḥadīth.

> ʿAbdullāh bin ʿAmr ibn al-ʿĀṣ (r) narrated: "I saw the Messenger of Allāh (s) counting *tasbīḥ* on his fingers (يعْقِدُ التَّسْبِيحَ)." (Nasā'ī)[20]

Making the *Adhkār* Audible

- **Audible *adhkār***: Although the *adhkār* after ending the ṣalāh may be done quietly, it is acceptable to do so slightly audibly. This is according to a number of ḥadīths by Ibn ʿAbbās (r).

> ʿAbdullāh ibn ʿAbbās (r) narrated: "At the time of the Messenger of Allāh (s), people would raise their voice with *dhikr* (رَفْعَ الصَّوْتِ بِالذِّكْرِ) after completing the obligatory prayers ... I would know by that when they finished (كُنْتُ أَعْلَمُ إِذَا انْصَرَفُوا بِذَلِكَ) when I heard it." (Bukhārī, Abū Dāwud)[21]

> ʿAbdullāh ibn ʿAbbās (r) narrated: "I used to know the completion of the ṣalāh of the Prophet (s) by (hearing) the *takbīr* (كُنْتُ أَعْرِفُ انْقِضَاءَ صَلَاةِ النَّبِيِّ ﷺ بِالتَّكْبِيرِ)." (Bukhārī, Muslim, Nasā'ī, Abū Dāwud)[22]

- **No textual reference requiring silent *adhkār***: The *Six Most Authentic Books* do not contain any Prophetic instruction that *adhkār* after the ṣalāh should be done quietly. Therefore, based on these ḥadīths above, it would be acceptable, if not recommended, to recite the *adhkār* in a way that is slightly audible.
- **Being considerate to others**: It is part of proper manner, however, that one does not recite *adhkār* too loudly in the *masjid* and disturb others who may be performing voluntary prayers or making up missed *rak'ahs*.

Raising the Hands in *Du'ā'* After the Ṣalāh

- **No textual reference**: The *Six Most Authentic Books* do not contain any ḥadīth that mentions that the Messenger of Allāh (s) used to raise his hands in *du'ā'* after performing the ṣalāh.
- **Raising the hands permissible**: Raising the hands in *du'ā'*, however, is permissible. There were instances when the Messenger of Allāh (s) raised his hands when making *du'ā'*, such as during the ṣalāh for rain, before the Battle of Badr, and so on. However, it was not his habit to do so after the daily prayers.
- ***Imām* representing others in *du'ā'***: Likewise, there is no evidence available for the *imām* to make *du'ā'* on behalf of the followers after the ṣalāh where the *imām* decides what to say or ask and the followers simply raise their hands.
- **Must have sincerity**: *Du'ā* should be made with humility and sincerity, and that is best done when one raises his hands to Allāh (swt) and directly expresses to Him (swt) what he wants from his heart, rather than another person doing it on his behalf. Making *du'ā'* once with sincerity from the heart is better than making it many times as a routine ritual without sincerity.
- For detailed discussions on these, see *Raising the Hands in Du'ā' After the Ṣalāh* on page 416 and *Imām Making Du'ā' After the Ṣalāh on Behalf of the Followers* on page 418 in the main book.

---

[1] Bukhārī, *Adhān*, 849.

[2] Abū Dāwud, *Ṣalāh*, 618, graded *ḥasan*.

[3] Al-Jazīrī, *Islamic Jurisprudence*, pp. 308, 311; Muḥammad and Mughniyyah, *Prescribed Prayers*, p. 48.

[4] Nasā'ī, *At-Taṭbīq*, 1143; *Forgetfulness*, 1320, 1323.

[5] Al-Jazīrī, *Islamic Jurisprudence*, pp. 308-09.

[6] Muslim, *Masājid*, 1315; Nasā'ī, *Forgetfulness*, 1318.

[7] Nasā'ī, *Forgetfulness*, 1324.

[8] Al-Jazīrī, *Islamic Jurisprudence*, p. 342. The Mālikī school consider the *taslīm* to be required only once to the right. For detailed positions of each school of thought, see pp. 309, 316, 322-23, 342-43.

[9] Nasā'ī, *Forgetfulness*, 1327.

[10] Muslim, *Ṣalāh*, 970; Nasā'ī, *Forgetfulness*, 1319; Abū Dāwud, *Ṣalāh*, 998-99.

[11] Al-Jazīrī, *Islamic Jurisprudence*, pp. 316, 344. In the Ḥanbalī school, the *taslīm* is for concluding the prayer, and is not a greeting. But if one has both intentions, then it is acceptable.

[12] Bukhārī, *Adhān*, 845.

[13] Bukhārī, *Adhān*, 846; *Istisqā*, 1038.

[14] Muslim, *Travellers*, 1642; Abū Dāwud, *Ṣalāh*, 615.

[15] Bukhārī, *Adhān*, 870, 875.

[16] Bukhārī, *Adhān*, 843; Muslim, *Masājid*, 1347-51; Nasā'ī, *Forgetfulness*, 1350; Ibn Mājah, *Establishing Ṣalāh*, 927.

[17] Muslim, *Masājid*, 1352-53; Abū Dāwud, *Witr*, 1504.

[18] Muslim, *Masājid*, 1334; Nasā'ī, *Forgetfulness*, 1338; Abū Dāwud, *Witr*, 1513; Ibn Mājah, *Establishing Ṣalāh*, 928; Tirmidhī, *Ṣalāh*, 300.

[19] Muslim, *Masājid*, 1334-35, 1337; Nasā'ī, *Forgetfulness*, 1338-39; Abū Dāwud, *Witr*, 1512-13; Ibn Mājah, *Establishing Ṣalāh*, 924, 928; Tirmidhī, *Ṣalāh*, 298-00.

[20] Nasā'ī, *Forgetfulness*, 1356.

[21] Bukhārī, *Adhān*, 841; Abū Dāwud, *Ṣalāh*, 1003.

[22] Bukhārī, *Adhān*, 842; Muslim, *Masājid*, 1316-18; Nasā'ī, *Forgetfulness*, 1336; Abū Dāwud, *Ṣalāh*, 1002.

Ṣalāh for Women

Some scholars are of the opinion that in certain areas of the ṣalāh, the postures of women are slightly different than those of men, such as how she raises her hands, where she places them, how she goes to the *sajdah*, how she sits, and so on. These are, however, *fiqhi* opinions that were derived based on the need for women's modesty. The entire collection of the *Six Most Authentic Books* do not contain any ḥadīth showing that there is any difference between men and women in how they perform the ṣalāh.

Women constitute half of the *ummah* of the Messenger of Allāh (s). Hence, it is reasonable to expect that he (s) would have informed his wives or the female Companions (r) if their ṣalāh posture needed to be different.

Al-Albānī, one of the foremost authorities in ḥadīth in our era, concluded:

> The description of the Prophet's (s) prayer applies equally to men and women, for there is nothing in the Sunnah to necessitate the exception of women from any of these descriptions. In fact, the generality of his (s) statement "pray as you have seen me praying" includes women.[1]

This is further supported by a ḥadīth by Umm ad-Dardā' (r). Imām Bukhārī reported in his *at-Tareekh as-Sagheer* that "she used to sit in her ṣalāh like a man sits, and she was a woman of understanding."[2]

While the physical postures in the ṣalāh may be the same for men and women, there are some valid differences in other aspects of the ṣalāh between men and women, such as her *ʿawrah*, going to the *masjid*, where she stands in the row while praying with other women, etc.

For a more detailed discussion on this topic, see *Ṣalāh for Women* on page 424 in the main book.

---

[1] Al-Albānī, *The Prophet's Prayer Described*, p. 93.

[2] Imām Bukhārī, *At-Tarīkh as-Saghīr*, vol. 1, p. 223.

Bibliography

ʿAlī, ʿAbdullāh Yūsuf, *The Meaning of the Holy Qur'ān*, Amana Publications, Beltsville, 1999.

Al-Albānī, Nāṣir ad-Dīn, *The Prophet's Prayer Described* (*Aṣlu Ṣifāt Ṣalat an-Nabī*), trans. Usama ibn Suhaib Ḥasan, Jāmiʿat Iḥyā Minhāj al-Sunnah, Suffolk, 2003.

Al-Bukhārī, Muḥammad ibn Ismāʿīl, *At-Tarīkh as-Saghīr*, Dār al-Maʿrifāh, Beirut, 1986, vol. 1, p. 223.

Al-Jawziyyah, Ibn Qayyim, *Ighatha al-Lufan fī Maṣāyiri ash-Shaiṭān*, Dār ibn al-Jawziyya, Cairo, vol. 1.

Al-Jazīrī, ʿAbd al-Raḥmān, *Islamic Jurisprudence According to the Four Sunni Schools,* (*Al Fiqh ʿAlā al-Madhāhib al-Arba'ah*), trans. Nancy Roberts, vol. I, Fons Vitae, Louisville, 2009.

Al-Misrī, Aḥmad ibn Naqib, *Reliance of the Traveller: A Classic Manual of Islamic Sacred Law* (*ʿUmdat as-Sālik wa ʿUddat an-Nāsik*), trans. Nuh Ha Mim Keller, Evanston, 1994.

Al-Musnad, Muhammad bin ʿAbdul-ʿAziz (Ed.), *Fatāwā Islāmiyah: Islamic Verdicts From the Noble Scholars ʿAbdullah bin Bāz, Ṣaliḥ al-ʿUthaymīn, ʿAbdur-Raḥmān al-Jibreen*, Darussalam, Riyadh, 2001, vol. 2.

An-Nīmawī, Muḥammad ibn ʿAlī, *Athar as-Sunan: The Book of Proofs for Purification and Prayer,* Turath Publishing, London, 2012.

Al-Zuhayly, Wahbah, *Al-Fiqh al-Islāmī wa Adillatuh*, Dār al-Fikr, Damascus, 1985, vol. 1 and 2.

Ibn Yusuf, Abdur-Rahman, *Fiqh al-Imam: Key Proofs in Hanafi Fiqh*, White Thread Press, Santa Barbara, 2003.

Jami' at-Tirmidhī, trans. Abū Khaliyl, Darussalam, Riyadh , 2007, vol. 1 to 6.

Muhammad, Allamah and Mughniyyah, Jawad, *Prescribed Prayers: A Textbook on Jurisprudence According to the Five Schools of Islamic Law*, Great Books of the Islamic World, Chicago, 2011.

Sabiq, As-Sayyid, *Fiqh us-Sunnah*, trans. Muhammad Sa'eed Dabas and Jamal al-Din M. Zarabozo, vol. 1, American Trust Publications, Indianapolis, 1991.

Ṣaḥīḥ al-Bukhārī, trans. Muhammad Muhsin Khan, Darussalam, Riyadh, 1997, vol. 1 to 9.

Ṣaḥīḥ Muslim, trans. Nasiruddin al-Khattab, Darussalam, Riyadh, 2007, vol. 1 to 7.

Sunan Abū Dāwud, trans. Yaser Qadhi, Darussalam, Riyadh, 2008, vol. 1 to 5.

Sunan an-Nasā'ī, trans. Nasiruddin al-Khattab, Darussalam, Riyadh, 2007, vol. 1 to 6.

Sunan Ibn Mājah, trans. Nasiruddin al-Khattab, Darussalam, Riyadh, 2007, vol. 1 to 5.

Glossary of Arabic Terms

(as). An abbreviation for the Arabic honorific *'alaihi-s-salām* (عليه السلام), meaning *peace be on him.*

(r). Abbreviation used in this work for honorifics after mentioning the name of a Companion of the Prophet Muḥammad (s). These are *raḍī allāhu 'anhu* ("may Allāh be pleased with him"), *raḍī allāhu 'anhā* ("may Allāh be pleased with her"), *raḍī allāhu 'anhum* ("may Allāh be pleased with them"), or *raḍī allāhu 'anhumā* ("may Allāh be pleased with them both"). Also used for *raḥimahu allāhu* or *raḥmatu allāhi 'alaihi*, meaning "may Allāh have mercy on him" when referring to a past Muslim, especially a prominent scholar.

(s). Abbreviation used in this work for the honorific *ṣallallāhu 'alaihi wa sallam* (صلى الله عليه وسلم), meaning "may Allāh's blessings and peace be upon him." This honorific is used anytime Prophet Muḥammad's (s) name is mentioned or referred to.

(swt). An abbreviation for the honorific *subḥānahu wa ta'ālā* (سبحانه و تعالى), meaning "may He be Glorified and Exalted", which is used when mentioning the name of Allāh (swt) or referring to Him (swt).

Adhkār. See *Dhikr*.

Al-Kutubu-s-Sittah (الكتب الستة). Also known as *Siḥāh Sittah* (صحاح ستہ). Lit. *The Authentic Six*. This refers to the six most authentic books of ḥadīth, namely Bukhārī, Muslim, Abū Dāwud, Tirmidhī, Nasā'ī, and Ibn Mājah.

Āmeen (آمين). The word that is usually uttered at the end of supplications or after reciting *sūrah* al-Fātiḥah. It means "Accept from me/us, O Allāh!"

'Aṣr (العصر). The third of the five daily obligatory prayers, which is offered at mid-afternoon.

'Awrah (عورة). Parts of the body of a Muslim man or woman that must be always covered.

Basmalah (البسملة). The Arabic text for *bismillāhi-r-raḥmāni-r-raḥīm* (بسم الله الرحمن الرحيم), meaning "In the Name of Allāh, the Most Merciful, the Most Compassionate."

Bid'ah (بدعة). Innovation in religion.

Da'eef (ضعيف). Means *weak.* A category of ḥadīth that is deemed to be defective in its chain, content, or other aspects.

Deen (دين). Commonly translated as *religion*, but more appropriately, *a way of life*.

Dhikr (ذكر). pl. *Adhkār* (أذكار). Invocation or words that glorify and praise Allāh (swt).

Du'ā' (دعاء). pl. *ad'iyah* (أدعية). Supplication or invocation to Allāh (swt). In this work, the word *du'ā's* is used for plural.

Fajr (الفجر). The first of the five obligatory prayers, which is offered at dawn.

Farḍ (فرض). Actions that are considered obligatory in Islamic jurisprudence. See *Wājib* to understand how the terms *farḍ* and *wājib* are interpreted by the four schools of thought.

Fātiḥah (الفاتحة). The opening *sūrah* of the Qur'ān, which is recited in all obligatory or voluntary prayers.

Fātiḥatu-l-Kitāb (فاتحة الكتاب). The *Opening of the Book*, or another name for *sūrah* al-Fātiḥah. It is also know as *Ummu-l-Kitāb,* or the *Mother of the Book.*

Fiqh (فقه). Islamic law or jurisprudence.

Ḥadīth (حديث). pl. *aḥādīth* (أحاديث). Sayings or actions of Prophet Muḥammad (s). In this work, the word *ḥadīths* is used for plural.

Ḥasan (حسن). Meaning *good.* In the context of ḥadīth literature, it refers to a type of ḥadīth that has a minor defect, making it short of being categorized as *ṣaḥīḥ* (authentic).

Iftirāsh (افتراش). Within the context of ṣalāh, it is a type of sitting in which one lays the left foot on the ground and sits on it, while the right foot is kept vertical with the toes facing the *qiblah.* One sits in this fashion during sitting in between the *sujūd* or in the first sitting in a three or four-*rak'ah* ṣalāh. See *Figure 8* on page 117 for illustration.

Imām (إمام). pl. *a'immah* (أئمة). Prayer leader. Also used as a title for a religious scholar. For example, the founder of each of the four schools of thought is called an "Imām." In this work, the word *imāms* is used for plural. When used as a title, the non-italic "Imām" is used.

'Ishā' (العشاء). The fifth of the five daily obligatory prayers, which is offered at night.

Iq'ā' (إقعاء). In the context of ṣalāh, a type of sitting in which one sits on the heels while keeping both feet vertical.

Jalsah (جلسة). Sitting position during the ṣalāh.

Jalsatu-l-Istirāḥah (جلسة الإستراحة). Sitting after the two *sajdahs* in the odd *rak'ahs* before standing up.

Julūsu-l-Awwal (الجلوس الأول). The first sitting after the 2nd *rak'ah* where one sits to recite the *tashahhud.*

Julūsu-l-Akhīr (الجلوس الأخير). The final sitting in the ṣalāh.

Jumu'ah (الجمعة). The Friday ṣalāh. Also, the name of the 62nd *sūrah* in the Qur'ān.

Khushū' (خشوع). Humility and awe of Allāh (swt) while making ṣalāh.

Madhhab (مذهب). School of thought. Pronounced *madh-hab.* pl. *madhāhib* (مذاهب). In this work, the word *madhhabs* is used for plural.

Madhāhib. See *Madhhab.*

Maghrib (المغرب). The fourth of the five daily obligatory prayers, which is offered at sunset.

Makruh (مكروه). An action that is disliked or detestable according to Islamic jurisprudence.

Marfū' (مَرْفُوْع). A category of ḥadīth in which the statement or the action is attributed to Prophet Muḥammad (s).

Masjid (مسجد). pl. *masājid* (مساجد). Place of worship where congregation prayers are held.

Mufaṣṣal (المفصل). Title given to the last sixty-five or sixty-six *sūrahs* in the Qur'ān that begin with *sūrah* 49 or 50. This is discussed in more detail on page 507 in the main book.

Musabbiḥāt (المسبِّحات). According to one interpretation, it is a title given to those seven *sūrahs* in the Qur'ān that begin with *sabbiḥ* (glorify) or one of its forms. See page 510 in the main book for more details.

Mutawātir (متواتر). A ḥadīth that is narrated by many Companions in such a multitude of narrations that its authenticity is beyond any doubt.

Mutawarrikan (متوركا). Meaning one sat in *tawarruk* fashion. See *Tawarruk*.

Qawmah (القومة). The standing position in ṣalāh after one rises from the *rukū'*.

Qiblah (القبلة). Direction to the Ka'bah in Makkah that one must turn towards when making ṣalāh.

Qiyām (قيام). Nightly voluntary ṣalāh. Also known as *tahajjud* (تهجد) ṣalāh.

Raf' al-Yadain (رفع اليدين). Literally means "raising both the hands", but specifically in the context of raising them before and after the *rukū'*.

Rak'ah (ركعة). pl *rak'āt* (ركعات). Unit of ṣalāh. Each standing portion of the ṣalāh is considered one *rak'ah*. Hence, the Fajr ṣalāh has two *rak'ahs*, Ẓuhr has four *rak'ahs*, Maghrib has three *rak'ahs*, and so on. In this work, the word *rak'ahs* is used for plural.

Rasūl (رسول). A *Messenger* sent by Allāh (swt) to guide people. Unlike a Prophet (*nabī*), a *Messenger* receives scripture from Allāh (swt).

Rukū' (ركوع). Bowing position in ṣalāh while holding on to the knees. See *Figure 4* on page 80 for illustration.

Ṣaḥīḥ (صحيح). A ḥadīth that has been categorized as *Authentic*.

Sajdah (سجدة). pl. *sujūd* (سُجود). The position of prostration in ṣalāh when one places his head on the ground while resting on the knees, hands, and the toes. See *Figure 7* on page 103 for illustration.

Ṣalāh (صلاة). pl. *ṣalawāt* (صلوات). Islamic ritual prayer. In this work, the word "prayers" is used for the plural.

Ṣalawāt. See *Ṣalāh*.

Shirk (شرك). Worshipping anything other than Allāh (swt) or associating any partner with Him (swt) or in His Attributes.

Siḥāh Sittah (صحاح ستة). See *Al-Kutubu-s-Sittah*.

Subḥ (الصبح). Another name for the Fajr or Dawn ṣalāh.

Sujūd. See *Sajdah*.

Sunnah (سنة). The collective body of the Prophet's (s) examples as recorded in the books of ḥadīths. In the Shāfi'ī and Ḥanbalī schools, the terms "sunnah", "recommended" and "desirable" mean the same. It is used for all voluntary and recommended acts that earns one extra rewards but omission does not incur any sin. Mālikī school have similar view, but they draw distinction between the Prophetic "sunnah" and other voluntary or "recommended" acts. (See al-Jazīrī, *Islamic Jurisprudence*, pp. 314, 347.) The word "sunnah" is also used for voluntary prayers that the Prophet (s) used to perform. In this work, the former is used with a capital "S" ("Sunnah") while the latter is used in italics (*sunnah*).

Sūrah (سورة). A division in the Qur'ān. It is often translated as "chapter", although it is not exactly the same.

Ta'awwudh (تعوذ). Seeking refuge in Allāh (swt) from the Satan by reciting a phrase, which is commonly, *a'ūdhu billāhi min ash-shayṭāni-r-rajīm* (أعوذ بالله من الشيطان الرجيم).

Tafsīr (تفسير). Qur'ānic exegesis or interpretation.

Tahajjud. See *Qiyām*.

Taḥiyyah (التحية). Another name for the *tashahhud*.

Taḥmīd (التحميد). In the context of the ritual ṣalāh, *taḥmīd* refers to the utterance of the phrase *rabbanā (wa) laka-l-ḥamd* ("Our Lord, to You is the praise") following the phrase *samiʿ allāhu liman ḥamidah* ("Allāh hears those who praise Him") when one rises up from the *rukūʿ*.

Tajwīd (تجويد). Rules of pronunciation and recitation of the Qur'ān. See also *Tartīl.*

Takbīr (تكبير). The phrase *allāhu akbar* ("Allāh is the Greatest").

Takbīratu-l-Iḥrām (تكبيرة الاحرام). The *opening takbīr*, or saying *allāhu akbar* when starting the ṣalāh.

Taqlīd (تقليد). Following a particular scholar's opinions without question and without examining the evidence for his opinions. Sometimes referred to as "blind following."

Tartīl (ترتيل). Recitation of the Qur'ān in slow, measured, rhythmic, and melodious tone. In the Qur'ān, Allāh (swt) instructs the Prophet (s) to recite the Qur'ān with *tartīl*: "and recite the Qur'ān in slow, measured rhythmic tones." (73:4) See also *Tajwīd.*

Tasbīḥ (تسبيح). A phrase for glorifying Allāh (swt), such as *subḥāna allāh* ("May Allāh be glorified").

Tashahhud (التشهُّد). Refers to the recitation of the *testimony* in the first and the final sitting in the ṣalāh, which begins with the words *at-taḥiyyātu.*

Taslīm (التسليم). The phrase *as-salāmu ʿalaikum wa raḥmatullāh* ("peace be upon you, and the Mercy of Allāh"). One ends the ṣalāh with this phrase in the final sitting. See *Figure 10* on page 140 for illustration.

Tasmīʿ (التسميع). In the context of the ṣalāh, *tasmīʿ* refers to the utterance of the phrase *samiʿ allāhu liman ḥamidah* ("Allāh hears those who praise Him") when one rises up from the *rukūʿ*.

Ṭawāf (طواف). Circumambulating around the Kaʿbah during *Ḥajj* or *ʿUmrah.*

Tawarruk (تورك).Within the context of ṣalāh, it is a type of sitting in which one sits on the left posterior while the right foot is kept vertical and the left foot extends from under the right leg. One sits in this fashion during the final sitting in the ṣalāh. See *Figure 9* on page 127 for illustration.

Tawfīq (توفيق). To be granted success by Allāh (swt) in a given task.

Ummah (أمة). The *Islamic Nation*, or the collective body of the entire Muslim population in the world.

Ummu-l-Qur'ān (أم القرآن). The *Mother of the Book*, or another name for *sūrah* al-Fātiḥah. It is also know as *Fātiḥatu-l-Kitāb,* or the *Opening of the Book*.

Wājib (واجب). A *duty* in Islamic jurisprudence. Ḥanafī and Ḥanbalī schools distinguish *farḍ* (obligatory) from *wājib*, which is less binding than *farḍ*. In their view, ṣalāh is still valid if one misses a *wājib* action unintentionally, but it will require a *sajdah* of forgetfulness after the *taslīm*. If it is omitted intentionally, then the ṣalāh needs to be repeated. If it is not repeated, then the ṣalāh is still valid but the person will be guilty of wrongdoing. In the Mālikī and Shāfiʿī schools, *farḍ* and *wājib* mean the same – obligatory. (See al-Jazīrī, *Islamic Jurisprudence*, pp. 310, 312.)

Wuḍū' (وضوء). Ablution or ritual purification that is necessary before performing ritual prayers.

Ẓuhr (الظهر).The second of the five daily obligatory prayers, which is offered at past noon.

Index

Companions and classic scholars' names appear as they are known to be; others are by last name.

ʿĀ'isha
- *basmalah* to be quiet, 44
- looking around during ṣalāh, 35
- manner of *rukūʿ*, 78
- manner of *sajdah*, 102
- opening *takbīr*, 28
- recitation in *qawmah* when following *imām*, 91
- reciting more than one *sūrah* in a *rakʿah*, 56
- reciting part of a *sūrah* in a *rakʿah*, 57
- reciting properly and skillfully, 67
- ṣalāh while sitting, 23, 26
- switching between sitting and standing, 26

ʿAbdullāh bin ʿAmr ibn al-ʿĀṣ
- counting *tasbīḥ* by finger, 144

ʿAbdullāh bin Mālik, 101

ʿAbdullāh ibn Masʿūd
- making personal *duʿā'* in final sitting, 135

ʿAlī ibn Abī Ṭālib
- heard him (s) saying *āmeen*, 50, 51
- no Qur'ān recitation in *rukūʿ/sajdah*, 86
- *taslīm* the final action in ṣalāh, 137

ʿAlqamah bin Waqqāṣ, 26

ʿAmr bin Ḥuraith
- recitation in Fajr, 69

ʿĀṣim bin Kulaib, 121

ʿAṣr
- beard moved with recitation, 70
- definition, 151
- recitation heard sometimes, 48, 54, 70
- recitation in first 2 *rakʿahs* only, 54, 58
- what is recited, 60

ʿAwrah, 151

ʿEīd
- audible recitation, 70
- length of recitation, 58
- what is recited, 61

ʿImrān bin Ḥuṣayn
- ṣalāh while sitting – half reward, 26
- ṣalāh while sitting or lying down, 22

ʿIshā'
- beautiful recitation by the Prophet (s), 67
- definition, 153
- recitation audible, 70
- what is recited, 60, 69

ʿUbādah bin as-Ṣāmit
- al-Fātiḥah is required, 47

ʿUmar ibn al-Khaṭṭāb
- *basmalah* not heard, 44
- reward depends on intention, 20
- ṣalāh starts with al-Fātiḥah, 44

ʿUqbah bin ʿĀmīr
- excellence of al-Falaq/an-Nās, 65
- recitation in *rukūʿ*, 85
- when recitation in *rukūʿ/sajdah* initiated, 84

ʿUthmān bin ʿAffān
- *basmalah* not heard, 44

Abū as-Sā'ib, 49

Abū Bakr as-Ṣiddīq

basmalah not heard, 44
ṣalāh starts with al-Fātiḥah, 44
Abū Ḥumaid as-Sā'idī
manner of *rukū'*, 76, 77, 78
manner of *sajdah*, 97, 99, 100, 102
manner of sitting between *sujūd*, 109
odd *rak'ah* - not sitting briefly, 113
raising hands at 3rd *rak'ah*, 123
raising hands to shoulders, 30
takbīr at 3rd *rak'ah*, 122
takbīr before/after *sajdah*, 111
Abū Hurairah
al-Fātiḥah in every *rak'ah*, 48
al-Fātiḥah required for ṣalāh, 47
basmalah recited, 43
consequence of going ahead of the *imām*, 30
do not go ahead of the *imām*, 29
facing *qiblah*, 21
going to *sajdah* – hands first, 95
making *du'ā'* in *sajdah*, 106
making personal *du'ā'* in final sitting, 135
opening *du'ā'* in first *rak'ah* only, 42
opening *takbīr*, 28
opening *takbīr* when following *imām*, 28
pause after opening *takbīr*, 40
raising hands during *rukū'*, 75
raising hands to shoulders, 31
recitation – consideration for people, 68
recitation – importance of understanding, 67
recitation in *qawmah* when following *imām*, 91
saying *āmeen*, 50, 51
seeking refuge, 129, 132
takbīr during *sajdah*, 109, 112
virtues of *āmeen*, 52
when *imām* recites, listen, 48, 59
Abū Mas'ūd al-Anṣārī
ṣalāh invalid if *rukū'* incorrect, 82
Abū Mūsā al-Ash'arī
saying *āmeen*, 51
takbīr when going to *sajdah*, 94
tashahhud, 118
when *imām* recites, listen, 48, 59
Abū Qatādah
al-Fātiḥah in every *rak'ah*, 48
quiet recitation in Ẓuhr/'Aṣr, 69, 70
recitation in 1st and 2nd *rak'ahs*, 54
recitation shorter in subsequent *rak'ahs*, 58
Abū Salāmah
recitation in 1st and 2nd *rak'ahs*, 54, 58
Abū Wā'il
reciting multiple *sūrahs* in a *rak'ah*, 56
Al-Albānī, Nāṣir ad-Dīn
āmeen to be loud and simultaneous with *imām*, 51
iftirāsh and *iq'ā'* both valid, 110
length of *rukū'/sajdah*, 83
on *iftirāsh/tawarruk* sitting, 126
on reciting Fātiḥah behind *imām*, 49
on ṣalāh of women, 147
placing hands first when going to *sajdah*, 95
placing hands on chest, 33
sajdah – forehead/nose to touch ground, 98
Al-Barā' bin 'Āzib
facing people after ṣalāh, 142
length of *rukū'/sajdah*, 83, 89
manner of *sajdah*, 100
recitation in 'Ishā', 69
reciting in beautiful voice, 67
Al-Kutubu-s-Sittah
also knows as *Siḥāh Sittah*, 155
definition, 151

Al-Mubārakfūrī, ʿAbd al-Raḥmān, 56
Āmeen
  arguments against saying loudly, 50
  definition, 151
  elongating it, 50
  heard *āmeen*, 50, 51
  meaning, 49
  raised voice with it, 50
  say after *wa lā-ḍ-ḍāllīn*, 51
  say when the *imām* says, 50
  scholars' opinions, 50
  simultaneously with the *imām*, 51
  stretched his voice with it, 50
  virtues of, 52
Anas bin Mālik
  basmalah not heard, 44
  imām should be followed, 29
  length of *rukūʿ/sajdah*, 89
  making *rukūʿ/sajdah* properly, 82
  manner of *sajdah*, 100
  not looking up during ṣalāh, 36
  opening *takbīr* when following *imām*, 29
  position of the feet, 23
  raising hands during *rukūʿ*, 75
  recitation – consideration for people, 68
  ṣalāh while sitting, 22
  ṣalāh while sitting – half reward, 25
  virtues of al-Ikhlāṣ, 64
An-Nuʿmān bin Bashīr
  position of the feet, 24

Basmalah
  definition, 152
  first verse of al-Fātiḥah, 46
  opened ṣalāh with, 43
  recited quietly, 44
  scholars' opinions, 44

Dajjāl
  protection by reciting al-Kahf, 63
  seeking refuge from, 133, 135
Day of Judgment
  Muslims recognized by traces of *sujūd*, 93

Fajr
  at Ḥudaibiyah after rainy night, 142
  definition, 152
  recitation audible, 70
  sequential recitation, 66
  what is recited, 56, 60, 69
Fātiḥatu-l-Kitāb
  definition, 152
  reciting in every *rakʿah*, 48, 54
Final Sitting
  duʿā's from the Sunnah, 133
  figure, 127
  manner of, 125
  personal *duʿā'*, 134
  recitations, 128
  recitations are quiet, 120
  ṣalāh on the Prophet, 129
  scholars' opinions, 126
  seeking refuge, 131
  tashahhud, 118, 128
First Sitting
  figure, 117
  manner of, 115
  raising hands when standing up, 123
  recitation, 118
  recitations are quiet, 120
  scholars' opinions, 126
  standing up, 113
  takbīr when standing up, 122
Furqān, 62

Hell
  seeking refuge from, 132, 135
Hellfire
  is forbidden to consume traces of *sujūd*, 93

Hereafter
- excellence of *sajdah*, 93

Ḥudhaifah
- length of *rukū'/sajdah*, 83
- long recitation in *tahajjud*, 55
- recitation with slow pace, 67

Ibn 'Abbās, 'Abdullāh
- *adhkār* after ṣalāh audible, 144
- *basmalah* recited, 43
- manner of *sajdah*, 97
- order of recitation, 66
- reciting part of a *sūrah* in a *rak'ah*, 56

Ibn 'Umar, 'Abdullāh
- avoiding painful postures, 18
- manner of *sajdah*, 98
- raising hands during *rukū'*, 74
- raising hands to shoulders, 31
- ṣalāh while sitting, 21
- *takbīr* while raising hands, 30
- *takbīrs* in ṣalāh, 74

Ibn Ḥajar al-'Asqālānī
- *tashahhud* of Ibn Mas'ūd preferred, 119

Ibn Kathīr, Ismā'īl
- on *mufaṣṣal sūrahs*, 56

Ibn Mas'ūd, 'Abdullāh
- manner of making *taslīm*, 138, 139
- multiple *sūrahs* in a *rak'ah*, 56
- *tashahhud*, 118, 128
- *tashahhud* to be quiet, 120

Iftirāsh
- definition, 18, 152
- figure, 117
- in between *sujūd*, 109
- in between *sujūd* – scholars' opinions, 110
- in first sitting, 115
- manner of, 109, 115

Imām Abū Ḥanīfah
- *basmalah* part of al-Fātiḥah, 44
- *iftirāsh* in all sittings, 126

Imām Aḥmad
- *basmalah* to be quiet, 45
- hands to be placed below chest, 33
- on *iftirāsh/tawarruk* sitting, 126
- *tashahhud* of Ibn 'Abbās preferred, 119

Imām Bukhārī
- ṣalāh of women, 147

Imām Mālik
- on *iftirāsh/tawarruk* sitting, 126

Imām Muslim, 119

Imām Nawawī
- how high the hands to be raised, 31
- prefers *tashahhud* of Ibn Mas'ūd, 119

Imām Shāfi'ī
- hands to be placed on or below chest, 33
- how hight the hands to be raised, 31
- on *iftirāsh/tawarruk* sitting, 126

Imām Tirmidhī
- prefers *tashahhud* of Ibn Mas'ūd, 119
- *sajdah* – arms to be away from sides, 101

Index Finger
- clenched other fingers, 120
- formed a circle, 121
- manner of raising – summary, 120
- to move or not, 121
- where to look, 122

Injīl, 62

Iq'ā'
- alternative to *iftirāsh*, 110
- definition, 153

Jābir bin 'Abdullāh
- best ṣalāh is with long recitation, 68
- excellence of al-Ikhlāṣ, 65
- facing *qiblah*, 21
- ṣalāh while sitting, 21

Jābir bin Samurah
whom to address during *taslīm*, 141
Jalsah, 109, 153
Jalsatu-l-istirāḥah, 19
Jalsatu-l-Istirāḥah, 112, 153
Jarīr Aḍ-Ḍabbī, 33
Jubair bin Muṭʿim, 69
Jumuʿah
what is recited, 61

Khabbāb bin al-Aratt
tongue moves during recitation, 70
Khushūʿ
avoiding painful positions, 17
definition, 153

Madhhab, 153
Maghrib
definition, 153
recitation audible, 70
splitting a *sūrah* between 2 *rakʿahs*, 57
what is recited, 60, 69
Maimunah bint al-Ḥārith
arms away from sides in *sajdah*, 101
Mālik bin Ḥuwairith
briefly sitting in odd *rakʿahs*, 112
raising hands to ears, 31
Marfūʿ, 153
Masjid
adhkār after ṣalāh, 145
definition, 154
excellence of al-Ikhlāṣ, 64
missed by ʿĀ'isha (r), 102
Mufaṣṣal
definition, 154
hasty recitation, 56
in Fajr, 60
in Maghrib, 60
in'Isha, 60
more than one *sūrah* in a *rakʿah*, 56
Mutawarrikān
definition, 154
sat in *tawarruk* at end of last two *rakʿahs*, 126
sat in *tawarruk* before *taslīm*, 126
Mutawātir
al-Fātiḥah required for ṣalāh, 47
definition, 154
facing the *qiblah*, 20
raising hands before/after *rukūʿ*, 74

Nuʿaim al-Mujmir
recited *basmalah* before al-Fātiḥah, 43

Opening *Duʿā'*
in first *rakʿah* only, 42
texts, 40
Opening *Takbīr*
pause after, 40
started ṣalāh with, 28
when following an *imām*, 28

Paradise
excellence of al-Ikhlāṣ, 64
excellence of *sujūd*, 93
Placing the feet, 23
Placing the hands
above the navel, 33
figure, 37
leaving them hanging, 35
manner of holding on chest, 34
on chest, 33
on chest (left side), 35
on ground before knees, 95
on ground during *sajdah*, 97, 98, 99
on knees during *rukūʿ*, 76, 77, 78
on knees during sitting, 121
on thighs during sitting, 115

Qawmah
definition, 154

length, 89
recitation, 89
recitation when following, 91
Qiblah
definition, 154
fingers during *sajdah*, 100
fingers to be in natural state during *sajdah*, 100
in obligatory ṣalāh, 21
required for ṣalāh, 20, 21
scholars' opinions, 21
toes during *sajdah*, 102
toes during *sajdah* – scholars' opinions, 102
toes during sitting, 115

Raf' al-Yadain
definition, 154
mutawātir ḥadīth, 74
supported by majority of scholars, 75
Raising the hands
before/after *rukū'*, 74, 75, 88
during opening *takbīr*, 30
figure, 32
in *du'ā'* after ṣalāh, 145
incorrect practices, 32
to ears, 31
to shoulders, 31
Recitation
adhkār after ṣalāh, 143
al-Fātiḥah, 47
beautifying recitation, 67
best ṣalāh with longer recitation, 68
consideration for people, 68
in final sitting - *du'ā's* from Sunnah, 133
in final sitting - personal *du'ā'*, 134
in final sitting - ṣalāh on the Prophet (s), 130
in final sitting - seeking refuge, 131
in *qawmah* - when following an *imām*, 91
in *rukū'*, 83
in *rukū'/sajdah* - how many times, 85
in *sajdah*, 105
minimum amount to recite, 57
recitation in 3rd/4th *rak'ah*, 55
recitation in first 2 *rak'ahs*, 54
reciting a complete *sūrah*, 55
reciting multiple *sūrahs*, 56
reciting part of a *sūrah*, 56
shorter in subsequent *rak'ahs*, 58
the *taslīm*, 138
tongue to move in quiet recitations, 70
when audible and quiet, 69
Rifā'ah bin Rāfi'
body must come to rest in all movements, 81
face firmly on ground during *sajdah*, 98
Rukū'
arms away from sides, 77
back/head in level, 78
being at ease, 81, 88
figure, 80
grabbing knees, 77
hands on knees, 76
hands to support body weight, 76
length, 83, 89
not reciting Qur'ān in, 85, 86
raising hands before/after, 74, 75, 88
recitation, 84
recitation – when initiated, 84
ṣalāh invalid if *rukū'* incorrect, 82, 104
takbīr before/after, 74
where to look, 78

Sa'd bin Abī Waqqāṣ
rukū' – placing hands on knees, 76

taslīm – turned fully, 139

Sabiq, As-Sayyid
āmeen to be loud and simultaneous with *imām*, 52
how high to raise the hands, 99
iftirāsh and '*iq'ā'* both valid, 110
Sahl bin Sa'd
how to hold hands, 34
Sajdah
arms away from sides, 101
being at ease, 81, 104
elbows above ground, 100
excellence of, 93
face firmly on ground, 98
feet vertical, 102
figure, 103
fingers towards *qiblah*, 100
going to sajdah - figure, 96
hands on ground, 98
length, 83, 89
making *du'ā'*, 93, 106
manner of the hands, 99
no Qur'ān recitation in, 85
nose/forehead on ground, 81, 97, 104
not reciting Qur'ān in, 86, 106
on seven bones, 97
place of focus, 122
placing hands first on ground, 95
recitation, 105
recitation – how many times, 85
recitation – when initiated, 84
ṣalāh invalid if *sajdah* incorrect, 82
standing up from sajdah/sitting - figure, 96
takbīr before/after, 94, 109, 111-12
thighs away from belly, 102
toes towards *qiblah*, 102
Samurah bin Jundub
facing people after ṣalāh, 141
two pauses in ṣalāh, 40
Seeking Refuge
during Qur'ān recitation, 67
in final sitting only, 129
ta'awwudh, 42
texts, 132
Sitting Between the *Sujūd*
being in full rest, 110
known as *jalsah*, 109
length, 110
recitation, 111
Sitting of Rest, 112
Subḥ
definition, 155
recitation shorter in 2nd *rak'ah*, 54, 58

Ta'awwudh
after opening *du'ā'*, 42
definition, 155
texts, 42, 43
Tahajjud
long recitation, 55
what is recited, 61
while sitting, 26
Taḥiyyah
definition, 155
Taḥmīd
definition, 155
recitation, 89
scholars' opinions, 91
when praying alone or leading as *imām*, 90
Tajwīd
definition, 156
elongating *wa lā-ḍ-ḍāllīn*, 51
etiquette of Qur'ān recitation, 67
Takbīratu-l-Iḥrām, 28
Taqlīd, 156
Tartīl
definition, 156
etiquette of Qur'ān recitation, 67

Tasbīḥ
counting by finger, 144
definition, 156
Tashahhud
definition, 156
index finger raised, 122
recited quietly, 119
scholars' opinions, 128
seek refuge after, 132, 135
text of Ibn Mas'ūd, 119
when to recite, 118
Taslīm
adding *wa barakatuh*, 138
definition, 156
du'ā' before *taslīm*, 134
figure, 140
final action in ṣalāh, 137
how much to turn, 139
text of the *taslīm*, 138
to the right, then left, 138, 139
whiteness of his cheek visible, 138, 139
whom to address, 140, 141
Tasmī'
definition, 156
recitation, 89
scholars' opinions, 91
when praying alone or leading as *imām*, 90
Ṭawāf, 156
what is recited, 61
Tawarruk
arguments against, 128
definition, 18, 156
figure, 127
in final sitting, 125
manner of, 113
Tawrah, 62
Ṭāwus
hands on chest, 33
sitting between *sujūd* - *iq'ā'*, 110

Ubay bin Ka'b
al-Fātiḥah – never been revealed before, 62
recitation in Witr, 66
Umm Salāmah
staying seated after ṣalāh, 137, 143
Ummah, 157
Ummu-l-Qur'ān
definition, 157
recitation in Ẓuhr and 'Aṣr, 54, 58
recited the *basmalah* before, 43
ṣalāh deficient without it, 47
ṣalāh invalid without it, 49

Wā'il bin Ḥujr
heard *āmeen*, 50
manner of holding the hands, 34
manner of *sajdah*, 99
raising hands during *rukū'*, 75
raising hands to shoulders, 31
stretched voice with *āmeen*, 50
Wuḍū'
definition, 157
perform properly, 21

Zabūr, 62
Zaid bin Khālid, 142
Ẓuhr
beard moved with recitation, 70
definition, 157
recitation heard sometimes, 48, 54, 69, 70
recitation in first 2 *rak'ahs* only, 54, 58
recitation shorter in 2nd *rak'ah*, 58
what is recited, 60

Lightning Source UK Ltd.
Milton Keynes UK
UKOW06f1427130515

251432UK00014B/121/P

9 781943 108022